CW01654160

Picture Show
Every Monday
2d.
April 5th. 1924.
Vol. 10.
No. 258.
How Felix the Cat is made to walk
SPECIAL ARTICLE
:: :: INSIDE. :: ::

POPEYE'S
CRUISE
SPINACH
I. M. HAPPY.

The Great

CARTOON STARS

A Who's Who

DENIS GIFFORD

JUPITER BOOKS

First published 1979
Jupiter Books (London) Limited
167 Hermitage Road, London N4 1LZ

SBN 904041 344

Text and this arrangement copyright © Jupiter Books (London) Limited 1979

© 1972 Walter Lantz PRODUCTIONS

Contents

Introduction

Felix keeps on walking, keeps on walking still...

And as long as there is the familiar flicker of light and clicking of sprocket-holes, Felix will keep on walking. He has already outlived his master, Pat Sullivan, by more than forty years, and, even if that doesn't qualify Felix the Cat for a niche in the movie hall of fame, then the laughter he continues to create most surely does.

Felix the Cat was the first cartoon superstar. His funny face and detachable tail have brought applause from audiences all around the world. His black blot of a body was as universal a figure of fun as Charlie Chaplin's tramp. Dolls, comics, books, toys, postcards, records – a host of spin-off figures walk behind the celluloid idol, for Felix was the first cartoon hero to experience exploitation. But though his figure may loom larger than any other on the silent screen, he was neither the first cartoon star, nor the first cartoon cat.

Felix was begotten of a long line of animated figures. Before him there was Bobby Bumps, and before Bobby there was Dreamy Dud, and before Dreamy there was Colonel Heeza Liar, and so the lineage rolls back with the years to Gertie the Dinosaur: you may see their genesis in the pages that follow.

As for specific precedents; before Felix came another of the genus *Felix felix* called Krazy. However Krazy Kat was already established as a comic strip hero before being signed for screen stardom by William Randolph Hearst (whose animation empire then amounted to a room or two full of ink-stained youngsters bossed by Gregory La Cava).

Though cartoons did not produce many superstars in the early days, they had been filmed since the start of the cinema. The first entertainment film ever made in England showed stage cartoonist Tom Merry whipping off a forty-second caricature of Kaiser Wilhelm. The following year, 1896, saw Georges Méliès in Paris and James Stuart Blackton in New York doing the same kind of thing. Even before the cinematograph was invented, Charles Emile Reynaud was giving animated cartoon shows in colour at his *Théâtre Optique* in the Paris of 1889. Packed audiences laughed at his story of *Poor Pierrot*, shown on a screen by his Projecting Praxinoscope. Cartoons can be traced even further back; through J. B. Linnett's flicker-book Kineograph of 1868, Joseph Plateau's revolving Phenakistiscope of 1833, Dr William Fitton's spinning Thaumatrope of 1819, back to Giovanni Della Porta's projection of a single sketch in his Black Chamber of 1558. But it was not until J. Stuart Blackton applied Méliès's method of making trick films to his own stage act of Lightning Cartoons that drawings first came alive on the cinema screen.

A little later, in France, Emile Courtet, a strip cartoonist who signed himself Emile Cohl, made the world's first fully animated cartoon film. Blackton's original attempt, *The Enchanted Drawing* (1900), had brought cartoons to life by means of careful cutting of the exposed film. He removed those parts which showed him drawing the changes in his pictures, so that it looked as if his funny faces changed expression of their own accord. Cohl devised a new method. He drew his film one picture at a time, and thus created a totally new art: the animated cartoon.

The resulting film, a two-minute item entitled *Fantasmagorie* (1908), was released in England as *Black and White*. 'Mysterious and humorous,' said the *Kinematograph Weekly*. 'It is an entire novelty and the humour is delightfully new. Price £2 net.' Mysterious and humorous it was indeed, with white lines on a blank screen forming themselves into little people watching a dancer do the high kick, while one angry patron rips up a lady's oversize hat.

The cartoon boom did not begin until five years later, however, but again Cohl was the creator. In the American studios of French Gaumont, he animated George McManus's popular comic strip, *The Newlyweds* (1913). The film was a hit

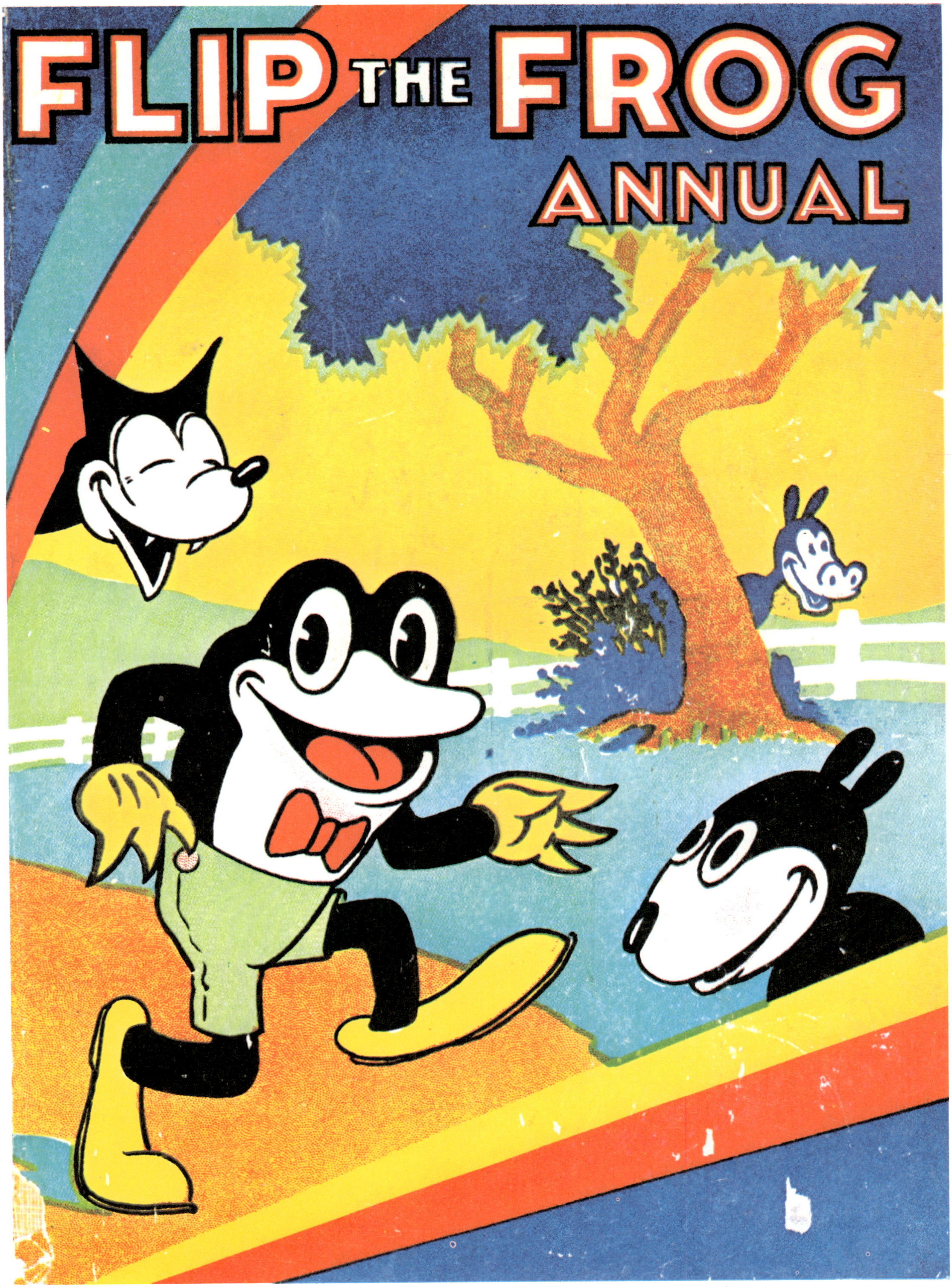
FLIP THE FROG
ANNUAL

because it had the one thing Cohl's previous cartoons had lacked – it had a hero. Mr and Mrs Newlywed's baby, Snookums, spoiled brat of the Sunday funnies, was a ready-made star with a million fans. They flocked to the nickelodeons to see him come to squalling life (the squalls, of course, were silent).

But while Cohl's new cartoon spun into a series that brought world attention to animation, he lost touch with that magical freedom of movement which had marked his early efforts. Snookums and his followers from the funny papers – and they were legion after Hearst's entry into animation – gave movies their cartoon stars, but they lost them the magic.

At this point, fortunately, Felix the Cat walks back into the picture. Pat Sullivan, himself a strip cartoonist of no low standing, created Felix for the screen in 1919. When he came over from the comics, Sullivan brought a bagfull of the funny gimmicks the strip artists had developed. Speech balloons, thinks bubbles, light bulbs to indicate ideas, storm clouds for despair: all were treated literally in Felix films, as were other comic strip clichés. When Felix looked daggers, he literally looked daggers – and their points came in handy to jab the enemy! From here Sullivan went on to develop new gimmicks. If a question mark could be drawn popping out of Felix's head, then it could just as easily be plucked physically from the sky and used as a handy hook, especially if a milk bottle stood just out of reach!

Thus Felix the Cat combined the continuing need for a cartoon hero with the fantastical freedom of the best animation. The combination was irresistible. Most of the cartoon stars who followed in Felix's footprints were cut to his pattern. Krazy Kat was revived in the Felix format, a far cry from Herriman's original. Paul Terry put black cats into his *Aesop's Fables* to plague the life of Farmer Al Falfa. And in Kansas City a young ex-ambulance driver called Walter Elias Disney gave a live-action girl a pussycat pal called Julius, and called the result *Alice in Cartoonland.* From this, his first series in 1924, Disney went on to create *Oswald the Lucky Rabbit* in 1927. Long ears apart, Oswald echoed the basic black blot form of Felix the Cat.
When the talkies came to town with Al Jolson, it may have been that old Jazz Singer's image that Hugh Harman and Rudolph Ising caricatured in their *Bosko the Talk-ink Kid* (1929), but the end product looked more like Felix minus his tail. Both Flip the Frog and the king of cartoon stars, Mickey Mouse, were copies of Felix in all but the carbon. But Mickey quickly developed a character and style all his own and, with the added attraction of a synchronised soundtrack, soon swept the screens of the world. The mouse had conquered the cat with her ready mouth and winning ways. The cheers that rocked the cinemas of our youth when Mickey's great face beamed from the screen still echo in memory when he turns up on television with his hearty 'Ha-ha!' and his 'Hey, Pluto!'

Walt Disney led the way through the thirties, thanks to his *Silly Symphonies* with their secret ingredient, Technicolour, but the Fleischers were not far behind. Brothers Max and Dave had struck a whole new vein of humour as early as 1918 by combining live action and animation in their trend-setting *Out of the Inkwell* cartoons: Koko the Clown clambering out of Max's inkpot and capering all over the screen was as mysterious and humorous as anything of Emile Cohl's. It was also in the thirties that cartoons came bang up to date by creating the first cartoon heroine, that thoroughly modern swinger, Betty Boop. With her saucy short skirt and her googoo eyes, Betty brought cartoons out of the kindergarten.

While the Fleischers pioneered the gag-packed cartoon for adults, Disney consolidated his crown as king of the kiddies' corner. His *Snow White and the Seven Dwarfs* (1937) was the world's first feature-length colour cartoon, an incredibly expensive gamble that eventually paid off. It also raised the cartoon film to the heights of art and further depressed the British animation industry. This continued to potter along with the occasional *Old Sam* or *Steve* short from Anson Dyer and Roland Davies, a disappointing sequel to a promising start in 1906 with pioneering conjurer Walter Booth and his *The Hand of the Artist.* England would not come into her own until the arrival of Bob Godfey's Biographic in the fifties, although there was brief, if derivative, delight in the *Animaland* cartoons produced by J. Arthur Rank in the forties.

The great watershed in the history of modern animation came in the post-war forties with the founding of United Productions of America by a crowd of dissenting Disneymen.

Taking over Columbia's Fox and Crow, and then creating their very own myopic Mr Magoo, UPA brought drawing back into cartoons. From UPA on, cartoon films no longer tried to imitate life. Cartoons once more were content to look like cartoons.

However, one legacy from UPA backfired to the detriment of animation. Their rule that only those parts of a drawing that had to move, should be moved, turned into the 'Law of Limited Animation'. From it has evolved not the stylish, cartoony quality UPA sought, but the corner-cutting, cost-dodging devices that have given the world the 'Television Cartoon', those static half-hours of close-up conversation where heads nod, eyes roll and any larger movement takes place off-screen with a cloud of stock dust and a shake of the camera. TV cartoons have created their own stars of course, but they are so far away from the Golden Age of Cartoon Heroes that they will not be found here – except for those few who have made it onto the big screen.

Ironically, it is the small screen that has saved the cartoon stars. Here the magic mouse still whistles up his wonders, and the sailor man who 'yam what he yam' still packs a punch which rocks parlour audiences. Porky Pig, Sylvester, Tweety Pie, Wile E. Coyote and Road Runner, not forgetting Tom the Cat and Jerry the Mouse, may have shrunk, but the gales of laughter they provoke are as strong as ever. In reputation, they stand undiminished. Come hell, high water, or Huckleberry Hound, the great cartoon heroes keep on walking.

Felix keeps on walking, keeps on walking still;
With his hands behind him,
You will always find him . . .

Animaland

England's only full-blown series of technicolor cartoons, produced by Walt Disney's ex-director David Hand at Moor Hall Studio, Cookham, for J. Arthur Rank's G.B. Animation unit. *The Lion* (1948) came first, then *The Cuckoo* and *The House Cat*, and in 1949 *The Platypus* and *The Ostrich*. A star was developed in *Ginger Nutt*, who featured in four films.

Alice in Wonderland

The self-possessed little English girl who followed a white rabbit to an undergound Wonderland. Heroine of Walt Disney's 75-minute cartoon released in 1951, 86 years after Lewis Carroll first published his novel, *Alice's Adventures in Wonderland*. Disney's adaptation includes episodes from Carroll's sequel, *Alice Through the Looking Glass*. The film's style is a streamlined version of the original illustrations by Sir John Tenniel. Alice was both modelled on and spoken by Kathryn Beaumont, a 12-year-old English actress, who also sang 'In A World Of My Own' and 'I Give Myself Very Good Advice' in the film. Producer: Ben Sharpsteen, Directors: Clyde Geronimi, Hamilton Luske, Wilfred Jackson.

Andy Panda

This cuddly black-and-white star of technicolour *Cartunes*, was created by Walter Lantz for Universal Pictures. Andy reflected the international ecstasy with which Ming the Giant Panda was greeted when he appeared at the London Zoo, pre World War II. Andy made his début in *Life Begins for Andy Panda* (1939), and one of his last appearances was in a walk-on guest spot in *The Woody Woodpecker Polka* (1951). Series directors: Burt Gillett, Alex Lovy, Dick Lundy.

© Walt Disney Productions

The Aristocats

Thomas O'Malley from the alley was the Don Juan of the dustbins and hep cat hero of *The Aristocats*, the 78-minute Walt Disney cartoon released in 1970. Our hero was spoken and, more importantly, sung by juicy-voiced Phil Harris; his lady-love, Duchess, by feline Eva Gabor. Her aristokittens were, Marie (Liz English), Toulouse (Gary Dubin) and Berlioz (Dean Clark). The Aristocats' title song was sung by the late Maurice Chevalier. Director: Wolfgang Reitherman.

Aesop

Ancient Aesop of Fable fame provided the title and theme for one of the longest running series in cartoons, *Aesop's Fables*. Paul Terry produced literally hundreds of these from 1920 into the Thirties.

Anson Dyer

E. Anson-Dyer, designer of stained glass windows, entered animation during World War I with *Dicky Dee's Cartoons* and became the nearest thing to a British Disney via his silent *Shakespeare Burlesques* and his sound and colour *Sam* series. Also many animated advertisements.

Baby Huey

This overgrown duckling was the biggest star, in physique, if not in reputation, to emerge from the Paramount-Famous Studios' *Noveltoons* of the fifties. With his pint-sized parents, Huey starred in such titles as *Huey's Ducky Daddy* (1953), under the direction of Seymour Kneitel. Quacked by Syd Raymond.

Baloo

Big, brown and happy-go-lucky, this bear was the protector of Mowgli in *Jungle Book* (1967), Walt Disney's adaptation of the Rudyard Kipling stories. Growling in the deep-fried, Southern tones of Phil Harris, Baloo stole the show when he carrolled out his philosophy in the song, 'The Bare Necessities' (written by Terry Gilkyson).

Bingo

Norman Cobb produced the first British series of sound cartoons beginning with *Bingo the Barking Baritone* (1930). Later Bingo's films were sold through Woolworth's for the Bingoscope home movie.

Bambi

This irresistible little deer rose from new-born fawn to Prince of the Forest in a brief 69 minutes. Walt Disney based *Bambi* (1942) on Felix Salten's novel, and after some six years in production, director David Hand came up with a cartoon masterpiece. Not only children cried when Bambi's mother was shot by Man, but with the coming of Spring, Bambi forgot sadness by falling antler over fetlock for the winsome Faline. The feature is considered by many to be Disney's most perfect cartoon.

Barney Bear

Brown bruin with an Edgar Kennedy slow-burn, Barney made his dozey début in *The Bear That Couldn't Sleep* (1939). Created for MGM by Rudolf Ising, Barney was taken over by Fred Quimby who gave him the voice of Paul Frees and starred him in films like *Bear Raid Warden*, a topical enough title at the time (1944). Barney's directors include Michael Lah and Preston Blair.

The Bearys

Charlie Beary is the domesticated dad of *The Beary's Family Album* (1963), a Walter Lantz *Cartune* series originally known by the title of *It's the Bearys.* To continue the pun fun, son Beary is called Chuck, and the family pet Goose Beary. Director: Paul J. Smith.

GEORGE
JOHN
SERGEANT PEPPER
THE APPLE BONKERS
THE SNAPPING TURTLE TURK
23
ROBIN THE BUTTERFLY STOMPER
BEA
YEL
SUBM

Beatles

The epoch-making Liverpudlian pop group were animated in *Yellow Submarine* (1968), an 87-minute musical cartoon made in England by Canadian director George Dunning to the stylish designs of the German Heinz Edelman. The Liverpool lads sang their own songs, but were given English speech by actors John Clive (John), Geoffrey Hughes (George), Lance Percival (Paul), and Paul Angelus (Ringo). The film is acclaimed by critics as a milestone in animation history.

Betty Boop

'You can feed me bread and water,
Or a great big bale of hay,
But don't take my boop-oop-a-doop
away!'

The censors tried to, but Betty Boop just rolled her great big googoo eyes, flipped her prototype mini, snapped a girlish garter, and won another million hearts. From the flirty thirties she tiptapped into the permissive seventies when a hundred of her black-and-white cartoons were reprocessed electronically into colour; and she won a million more hearts through TV. Created by Grim Natwick for Max Fleischer's *Talkartoons*, Betty was based on Helen Kane, the original boop-a-doop singer, and given voice by Mae Questal. The songs that scattered her series were written by Sam Lerner and Sammy Timberg, and she was often supported by such singing stars as Louis Armstrong, Cab Calloway, Maurice Chevalier, Fanny Brice, Rubinoff and his Violin, and the Royal Samoans. Titles include *Betty Boop for President* (1932), and in later movies she met such comic strip stars as The Little King, Henry, and Little Jimmy. She also 'introduced' Popeye and Sally Swing, the hep chick who usurped her throne.

Bimbo

Betty Boop's pet dog suffered quite a comedown; Betty was originally his girlfriend! Bimbo and Betty were the canine co-stars of the early *Talkartoons*, made by Max and Dave Fleischer. It's small wonder that in later films Bimbo changed his name to Pudgy, but he found some consolation when his starring vehicle *Riding the Rails* (1938) was nominated for an Oscar.

Beaky Buzzard

Bashful bird created by Bob Clampett for *Bugs Bunny Gets the Boid*, a Looney Tune of 1942. Beaky's voice by Kent Rogers.

Bluto

Popeye's perennial opponent, the brutal Bluto, stemmed directly from Elzie Segar's comic strip *Thimble Theatre* (1938). But while he appeared in only one strip sequence, he stayed in the Max Fleischer cartoons right to the bitter end, despite a sea-change to Brutus for the television series. Bluto's original voice was that of Gus Wicki; his best-known voice, Jackson Beck.

Big Bad Wolf

'Who's afraid of the Big Bad Wolf?' – as we all know, it certainly wasn't the porcine heroes of *The Three Little Pigs* (1933), the famous Walt Disney *Silly Symphony* in which the Big Bad Wolf, as ever, huffed and puffed and blew houses down. His huffing and puffing was dubbed on by voice-man Billy Bletcher. Having helped win Disney the Academy Award, B.B.W. returned in his own starring vehicle, *The Big Bad Wolf* (1935), then as the fearsome father in *The Three Little Wolves* (1935), and finally as the baddie in *The Practical Pig* (1939).

Bobby Bumps

Early star of the silent cartoon and the first cartoon hero to act exactly what he was, Bobby Bumps was a normal boy who got into normal scrapes. Created by newspaper strip cartoonist Earl Hurd, Bobby made his début for Joker Films with *Bobby Bumps Gets Pa's Goat* (1915). He appeared in more than 50 shorts over the following five years. Earl Hurd invented the Double Strip or 'cel' method of animation, which separated the drawing of the moving character from a permanent background – a system followed to this day.

THRILLING SCENES FROM THE BOOB WEEKLY

Done by R. L. Goldberg for Pathe.

SIMP CITY, TEXAS.
One-week-old son of Mr. and Mrs. Hannibal M. Sawdust, showing the result of the new scientific method of bringing up a child on powdered pool balls and sterilized bayrum. At the age of one week, this infant uses a safety razor and plays a good game of pinochle.

SOUPBONE, MINN.
Dedication of the monument to Olaf J. Ivory, the only honest lawyer in the United States. He starved to death. Miss Marjorie Jams, daughter of Jim Jams, mayor of Soupbone, hung a wreath of spinach and asparagus over the monument at the unveiling.

CONSTANTINOPLE, TURKEY.
When the city was in danger of capture by the Allies, the Sultan fled from the city with 831 of his wives and left the other 972 in the harem to feed the cat.

CHEESECAKE, N. Y.
Congressman John T. Blowhard reviews the youngsters of the A. D. T., the Association of Federated Messenger Boys, at their annual parade. The parade was 8 hours in passing.

CONSTANTINOPLE, TURKEY.
An intimate view of Koochie Koochie Gaflooie Pizazza, the Sultan's favorite, about to enter her marble bath for the morning dip.

LATE STYLES
Paris Fashions Direct from Hoboken: Something smart and snappy to be worn while being beaten by your husband.

Boob Weekly

Burlesque newsreel created in 1916 by Rube Goldberg, the fabled American comic artist after whom the Reuben Award is named.

Bongo

Bongo the Wonder Bear from the circus, with his girlfriend Lulubelle and his rival Lumpjaw, was created by novelist Sinclair Lewis. Walt Disney brought him to the screen as part of the 73-minute feature *Fun and Fancy Free* (1947) directed by Jack Kinney. Dinah Shore crooned Bongo's theme song, 'A Bear Likes To Say It With A Slap', while his story was narrated by Jimmy Cricket (Cliff Edwards).

Brer Rabbit

The fabulous folk-hero of Joel Chandler Harris's *Tales of Uncle Remus* was first animated in the silent era by England's Anson Dyer, but achieved movie immortality in the version inserted by Walt Disney into his live-action feature, *Song of the South* (1946). Jolly James Baskett played the Uncle Remus who told his tall tales to awestruck Bobby Driscoll and Luana Patten, while Wilfred Jackson directed these cartoon sequences. Brer Rabbit sang 'Zip-a-dee Doo-dah' by Allie Wrubel and Ray Gilbert, and his voice (Johnny Lee) helped win the song the Academy Award. James Baskett also did the voice of Brer Fox, while Brer Bear was Nicodemus Stewart.

Bosko

Almost an animated inkblot topped off with a bowler hat, this piccaninny starred as Bosko the Talk-ink Kid in Warner Brothers' first ever sound cartoon, *Sinking in the Bathtub* (1930). This was also the first *Looney Tune.* Bosko and his girlfriend Honey were created by Hugh Harman and Rudolf Ising, with Isadore (Friz) Freleng as main animator. His name was billed in the titles of 28 cartoons before Harman and Ising left Warners for MGM. They took Bosko with them, and smoothed him into a suitably cuter character for *Bosko's Parlor Pranks* (1934) and the films that followed.

Bonzo

This spotted-dog star, was the only British cartoon hero to sustain a full series of 26 films – no mean achievement in the silent days of 1924–1926. Bonzo was already an established star of comics, strips, magazines, postcards and ashtrays, when his creator George E. (for Ernest) Studdy brought him to the screen. Studdy had dabbled in animation as early as 1914 (*Studdy's War Studies*), and the Bonzo cartoons were made in close collaboration with his director William A. Ward. Writers included Adrian Brunel, later a major movie director, and animators included Brian White, later the creator of the popular Nipper strip.

Bubble & Squeak

Bubble, the driver, and Squeak, the baby taxicab, wheeled their way through a short series of British colour cartoons, steered by producer George Moreno, a former Fleischer animator, and driven by director Harold F. Mack. The first of their British Animated Productions was called *The Big City* (1946), but despite some merchandising, including a series of 'Bubble & Squeak' annuals, the characters failed to click.

Buddy

This bright boy took over *Looney Tunes* cartoons after Bosko left Warner Brothers for the plusher cels of MGM. Virtually a reversal of black boy Bosko, Buddy began under Leon Schlesinger's aegis with *Buddy's Day Out* (1933), ending his career 22 titles later with *Buddy the G Man* (1935). His voice was that of Jack Carr, and his directors included Jack King and Ben Hardaway.

Bugs Bunny

The rabid carrot-crazy rabbit with the catchphrase, 'Eh-h-h-h, what's up, Doc?' can claim four fathers. His immediate ancestor was Max Hare, star of Disney's *The Tortoise and the Hare* (1934). Bob Clampett created the first Warner Brothers bunny for *Porky's Hare Hunt* (1938), and director Ben Hardaway elaborated him, calling him 'Bug's Bunny' (Ben's own nickname was 'Bugs'). Chuck Jones used him in *Elmer's Candid Camera* (1940), and he finally bounced into stardom, complete with 'What's up, Doc?' in Tex Avery's *A Wild Hare* (1940). By 1962 Bugs had made 159 films, including the stereoscopic *Lumberjack Rabbit* (1953). He won the Academy Award for *Knighty Knight Bugs* (1958), directed by Friz Freleng. His voice, of course, is provided by the amazing Mel Blanc.

Buzz Buzzard

Big-beaked birdbrain who provided ideal opposition to smart-alec star Woody Woodpecker in the Walter Lantz *Cartunes*, Buzz made an early appearance in *Drooler's Delight* (1949) under the direction of Dick Lundy and the animation of Ben Hardaway. His voice: Dal McKennon.

Buzzy the Crow

A little black crow with a big brown voice, Buzzy brought out the best in Brooklyn-ese from Jackson Beck. He originally emerged from the Paramount *Noveltoons* series to star in *Stupidstitious Cat* (1954) and other such punny pictures. Directed by Seymour Kneitel, Buzzy's animators include Dave Tendlar and Larz Bourne.

LEON SCHLESINGER
Presents
THE NEW CARTOON SENSATION
"BUGS BUNNY"
Now Appearing In
LOONEY TUNES
and
MERRIE
RELEASED BY
NOTE
MODEL SHEET
M.M.22.

Bringing up Father

Perhaps more correctly entered under the names of 'Jiggs and Maggie', this famous newspaper strip by George McManus was animated into a cartoon series by Frank Moser for W. R. Hearst's International Film Service: *Bringing up Father* (1916).

REEL INCIDENTS CAUGHT FOR CANIMATED NOOZ

Done for Essanay by Wallace Carlson

Mr. and Mrs. Vernon Shanty illustrating for Canimated Nooz how to "Walk the Bow-Wow."

Miss Stake, society favorite, makes pet of monkey which appears on right of picture.

John Robbafeller makes a donation toward building a home for the homeless bar-flies.

Mr. Robbafeller then orders his secretary to see that gasoline is raised two cents.

Ball-room skating threatens to supplant dancing as the king of the indoor sports.

Doodabs, correspondent of Canimated Nooz, interviewing General Frank Fuster on border.

Canimated Nooz

This burlesque newsreel cartoon was created and animated by Wallace A. Carlson for the Essanay Company in the early silent days. The series was released regularly through 1915–1917, and sometimes featured Carlson's main hero, Dreamy Dud. Carlson later returned to the newspaper strips where he began, creating the long-running family saga, *The Nebbs* (1923).

Captain Hook

Elegant and evil, this one-handed pirate chief was created by Sir James Barrie in his play *Peter Pan* and remains the greatest villain in children's theatre. When Walt Disney produced his animated adaptation in 1953, Hans Conreid, the film actor, both modelled and declaimed the character. He also sang his own signature song, 'The Elegant Captain Hook', written by Sammy Cahn and Sammy Fain. *Peter Pan* was directed by Hamilton Luske, Clyde Geronimi and Wilfred Jackson.

Casey

Our deathless hero was first celebrated in a deathless poem, ('The outlook wasn't brilliant for the Mudville Nine that day; the score stood four to two with but one inning more to play . . .') by Ernest Lawrence Thayer. Jerry Colonna belted out the ballad 'Casey At The Bat' as part of the Walt Disney feature *Make Mine Music* (1946). Jack Kinney directed this Gay Nineties saga of baseball, and eight years later the free-swinging Casey struck (out) again in *Casey Bats Again*.

Casey Junior

No relation to Casey of baseball fame (above), Casey Junior was the little steam engine who 'thought he could' and did draw the circus train in *Dumbo*, Walt Disney's feature for 1941. He chuffed merrily to his own theme tune 'Casey Junior's comin' down the track, woo-woo . . .', written by Oliver Wallace and Frank Churchill.

Casper

Casper the Friendly Ghost, to give him his full title, is the guiding spirit of 52 cartoons from Paramount-Famous Studios, directed by Seymour Kneitel. In *Boo Bop* (1957), he helps Franz Schubert finish his 'Unfinished Symphony', and he once appeared in full 3-D in *Boo Moon* (1954). Casper's voice was Mae Questal right from the first film which was *Casper's Spree Under the Sea* (1950).

The Colonel

Monocled mouse created by George Moreno Jr for his British Animated Productions. The Colonel put paid to the Loch Ness Monster in *Loch Ness Legend* and to Frankie Stein in *The Old Manor House* (1948), directed by Harold Mack.

Charley

This archetypal hard-working good citizen, the very British hero of seven shorts sponsored by the Central Office of Information between 1947 and 1949, was created by John Halas and scripted by Joy Batchelor. He made his début in *New Town*, and in time there came a *Charley Jr*.

Charlie

Looking suspiciously like Charlie Chaplin, so suspiciously that cautious British distributors rechristened him 'Chum', Charlie starred in a string of cartoons made by Pat Sullivan in his pre Felix the Cat days. The first bore the catchy, almost catch-penny, title of *How Charlie Captured the Kaiser* (1918) and was distributed by Universal Pictures.

Charlie Brown

'Good Ol' Charlie Brown' – as he is known to his comic contemporaries, Linus, Lucy Van Pelt, and the rest of the kids who people the *Peanuts* strip created by Charles M. Schulz – came to the movies via television specials. He started in *A Boy Named Charlie Brown* (1970), with a voice dubbed on by Peter Robbins. Director Bill Melendez also made the 1972 sequel, *Snoopy Come Home*.

Charlotte

The spidery star of *Charlotte's Web* (1972) was adapted from E. B. White's novel by producers William Hanna and Joseph Barbera, taking time out from their television series to return to the cinema screen. Charlotte's voice was provided by the star of many a movie musical, Debbie Reynolds. The feature was directed by Charles A. Nichols and Iwao Takamoto.

Chester Cat

The house-cat star of a film baldly entitled *The House Cat* was an early 1948 entry in the *Animaland* series by J. Arthur Rank's newly-established studio, Gaumont British Animation. It was directed by Bert Felstead under the guidance of Disney producer David Hand.

Chilly Willy

Pocket-sized penguin who made his début in the epic *Chilly Willy* (1956). Subtitled *The Cold-blooded Penguin*, Willy spends his 6-minute segments snatching fish from under the protective nose of a dog named Smedly. Created by Walter Lantz for his Universal *Cartunes*, Willy was developed by Tex Avery into a silent star: like Dopey, 'he don't talk none'.

Cheerio Chums

Two ex-service comrades created by early English animator Dudley Buxton. Three adventures in civil commerce were included in the *Phillips Philm Phables* series (1919).

Chuck Jones

One of the most creative and innovative animator/directors, Charles M. Jones was born in Spokane in 1912. Began as a cell washer for Ub Iwerks on *Flip the Frog*, his first cartoon as director was *The Night Watchman* (1938). Most notable of many creation: *Road Runner*. Oscars: *For Sentimental Reasons* (1949), *The Dot and the Line* (1965), *Christmas Carol* (1974).

Chip 'n' Dale

Chattering chipmunks, Chip the cheery and Dale the dopey are the nut-hunting bane of Donald Duck's existence. Their début in *Squatter's Rights* (1946), directed by Jack Hannah and written by Harry Reeves and Rex Cox, was such a success that the short was promptly nominated for an Academy Award. So was their first title-starring film, *Chip an' Dale* (1947). The rapid-talking pair went into Cinemascope with *Chips Ahoy* (1956).

Clint Clobber

The hulky handyman who narrowly missed being a bear, retains the hairier characteristics of that lovable genus. Full name, DeWitt Clinton Clobber; full title, Superintendent and Sanitary Engineer of the Flamboyant Arms, a broken-down boarding house. Created by Gene Deitch for seven 'new look' *Terrytoons*, the S. & S.E. made his début in *Clint Clobber's Cat* (1957), and was spoken by Allen Swift.

Clarabelle

Unlikely but apparently compatible sweetheart of Horace Horsecollar, Clarabelle was an early member of the Walt Disney–Mickey Mouse Stock Company. Indeed, she was there in spirit if not in fact, right from the start; for Mickey, in *Steamboat Willie* (1928), plays a cow by the udder. However, this portion of Clarabell's anatomy so discontented censors that in later appearances she was forced to wear a skirt.

Clara Cluck

'Madame' Clara Cluck, as she was fully styled, was the operatic chicken whose guest-star appearances in such shorts as *Orphans' Benefit* (1934) and *Mickey's Grand Opera* (1936) rightly earned her the immortal billing, 'The Barnyard Nightingale'. Clara was clucked by Florence Gill, who appeared as herself in full cry in *The Reluctant Dragon* (1941).

Col. Heeza Liar

One of the earliest cartoon stars, Col. Heeza Liar's fabulous exploits outdid those of that other famous American explorer, President Theodore Roosevelt, upon whom he was based. Created by John Randolph Bray, pioneer American animator, he made his first expedition in *Colonel Heeza Liar in Africa* (1913), and pursued similar adventures a decade later in *Colonel Heeza Liar in the African Jungles* (1923), under the direction of Vernon Stallings. J. R. Bray was the silent era's equivalent of Walt Disney, organising an efficient studio operation and producing cartoons in regular series as weekly releases. With Earl Hurd he developed and co-patented the 'cel' process that considerably simplified the work of the animator.

Corny Crow

Corny's raucous squawk was first heard in *It's a Lovely Day* (1949), directed by Bert Felstead and produced by David Hand in the *Animaland* series of cartoons for J. Arthur Rank. He reappeared in *Ginger Nutt's Christmas Circus* (1949).

Daffy Duck

This little quacker made his début in *Porky's Duck Hunt*, a Warner Brothers *Looney Tune* produced by Leon Schlesinger in 1937. At the time, his creator, Tex Avery, called him simply 'The Crazy Darnfool Duck'. Such was his scatty impact that he rocketed to stardom in *Daffy Duck and Egghead*, made in the same year. His voice, originally based on film star Hugh ('Woo-Woo') Herbert, was later given a raspberry lisp by the astounding Mel Blanc. Chuck Jones developed Daffy through a sequence of detective and heroic roles to the fantastic apogee of *Duck Amuck* (1952), his wildest outing.

Cuckoo

Overweight star of, appropriately enough, *The Cuckoo* (1947), this character was given the name of 'Cooky' by those exploiters whose job it was to merchandise the David Hand *Animaland* cartoons.

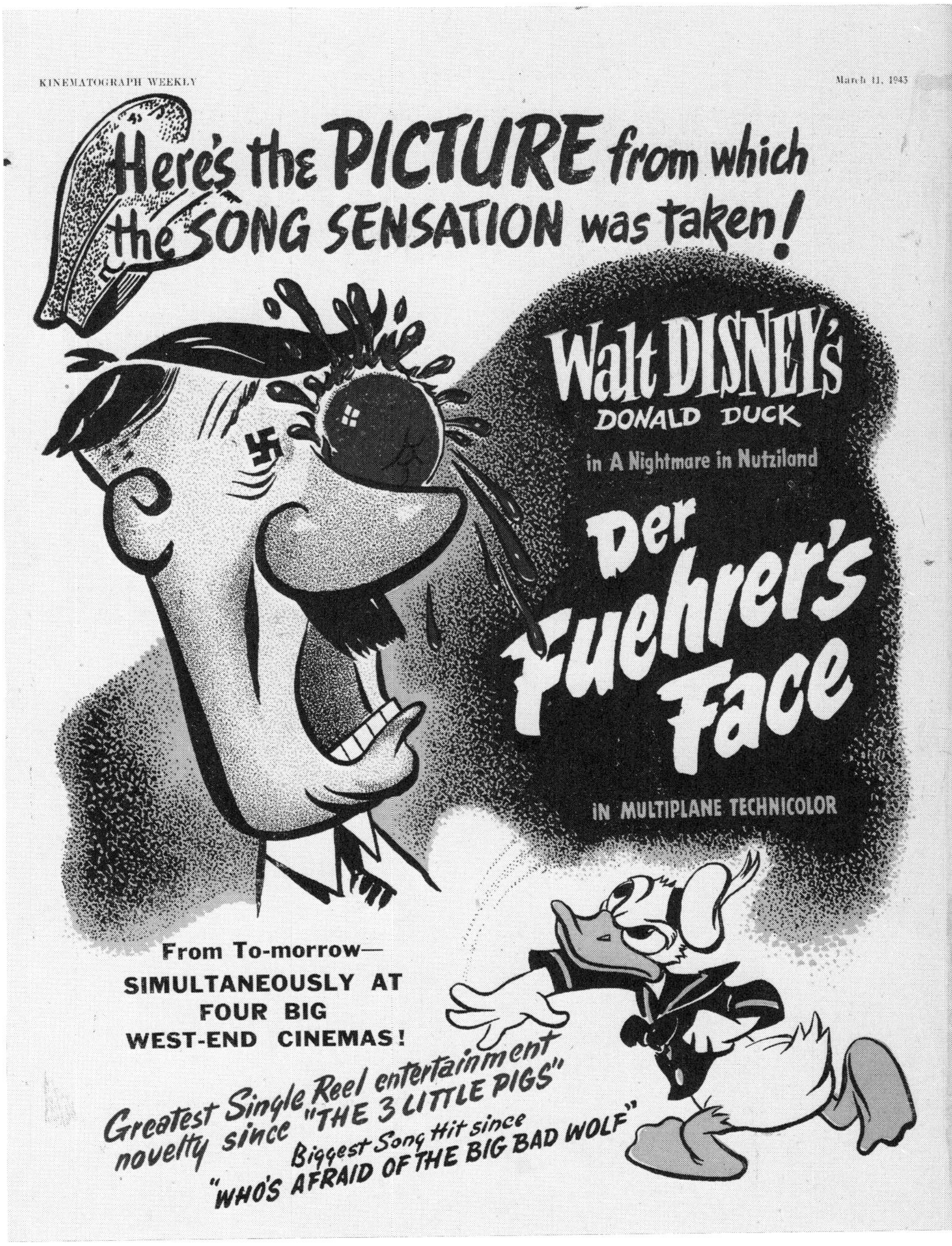

Donald Duck

'I wanna fight!' Donald's bellicose catchphrase quickly caught on with cinema-goers, thanks to the incredible squawk created for him by Clarence Nash. Donald started out as a supporting character in the Walt Disney *Silly Symphony* short, *The Wise Little Hen* (1934), then turned up to recite 'Mary Had A Little Lamb' to a mass of mice in *The Orphans' Benefit*, just three releases later. An instant hit, he shared star billing for the first time in *Donald and Pluto* (1936) and eventually won the Academy Award with *Der Fuhrer's Face* (1942). His swansong was *The Litterbug* (1961).

Daisy Duck

Donald Duck's fine feathered friend, Daisy was born, Donna Duck, the Mexican senorita of *Don Donald* (1936), under the direction of Ben Sharpsteen. After her Americanization, Daisy made her most telling appearance in *Donald's Dilemma* (1947), directed by Jack King.

Dinky Duck

A little black duckling this time from the *Terrytoon* farmyard, producer Paul Terry supervised Dinky's début in *The Orphan Duck* (1939), directed by Connie Rasinski (whose real name was Conrad). Dinky's quacks were supplied by story man Tom Morrison.

Deputy Dawg

The lazy lawman from *Terrytoon* country created by Larz Bourne and seldom seen without his slightly quicker-witted sidekicks, Musky Muskrat and Vincent Van Gopher. The deputy starred in 52 films beginning with *The Yoke's On You* (1960) and including one which marked the first appearance of *The Astronut* (1962), who span off into a television series of his own. Deputy Dawg's voice: Dayton Allen, suh!

Dreamy Dud

Dreamy Dud dreamed dreams that were anything but dud, in the company of Wags, his pet dog. They were creations of newspaper strip artist Wallace A. Carlson, and appeared in 28 cartoon films produced by him during 1915–16, starting with *A Visit to the Zoo*. He revived them in 1919 for his *Us Fellers* series, and they also turned up in short items for his *Canimated Noos Pictorial*.

Droopy

'Hello, folks. I'm the hee-ro!' – true enough words. This half-pint hound, whose droopy eyes hooded an undrooping heart, was created by Tex Avery for the MGM cartoon *Dumb Hounded* (1943). He shot to stardom, thanks in large part to the very funny voice given to him by Bill Thompson, who played Wallace Wimple in the radio series *Fibber McGee and Molly*. Droopy's sawn-off, stoical stance stood him in ideal stead as opposition to Tex Avery's wild Wolf, villain of such epics as *North West Hounded Police* (1946), written by Heck Allen. His tiny figure also made unusual use of the outsize cinemascope screen in *Millionaire Droopy* (1956).

Dinkum

Dinkum was the duckbilled girlfriend of Digger the duckbilled platypus. These Australian animals co-starred in one of David Hand's *Animaland* cartoons, *The Platypus*, released in 1948. They returned for guest-star roles in *Ginger Nutt's Christmas Circus* (1949).

Dumbo

'I think I seen about ever'thing when I see an elephant fly!' So sang Cliff (Ukelele Ike) Edwards and the coal-black Crows chorus. The rest of the world joined in when Dumbo stretched out his jumbo-sized ears and took off. The baby elephant that learned to fly was the star of *Dumbo* (1941), a short (64-minute) but sweet feature film from Walt Disney. Ben Sharpsteen directed from Dick Huemer's adaptation of the book by Helen Aberson and Harold Pearl. Most famous sequence: when Dumbo takes a drink and sees 'Pink Elephants On Parade'.

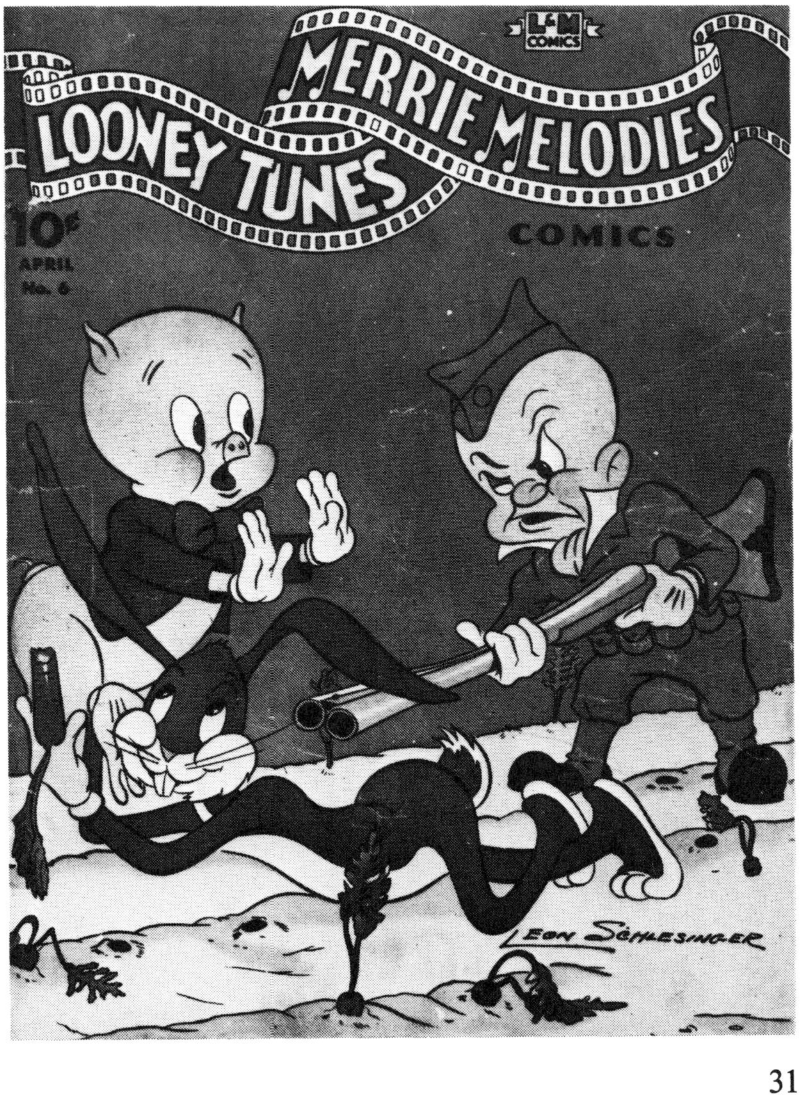

Elmer Fudd

Unwuffled wabbit hunter of many a *Merrie Melody*, this bald-pated hero owes much to the impedimented speech supplied by radio actor Arthur Q. Bryan. He was created by Tex Avery as one half of the 1937 Leon Schlesinger *Daffy Duck and Egghead* (the other half of the title is dealt with under 'D'!). Egghead was rechristened 'Elmer Dudd' in *A Feud There Was* (1938), but soon settled down as fuddy-duddy Fudd. Regular opposition to Bugs Bunny and Daffy Duck, Elmer was ultimately edged out by Porky Pig.

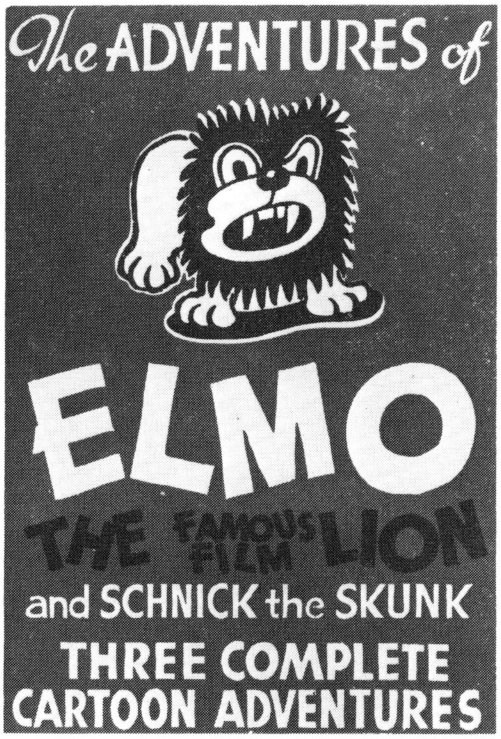

Farmer Al Falfa

This perpetual son of soil and toil made his début way back in 1915. Paul Terry created him for *Down on Phoney Farm*, then, as was Terry's wont, kept the poor old gaffer hard at it for more than 40 years. Small wonder that in later *Terrytoons* he changed his name to Farmer Gray. This hard labourer turned up as support to such farmyard stars as Gandy Goose and Kiko the Kangaroo.

Elmo

Elmo, the Famous Film Lion, so claimed his creator Charles Cole, of 'Magic Chalks' renown. Every history needs a mystery, and this is ours. A weekly strip and a couple of comics perpetuated Cole's claim but no actual film has ever been traced. Cole changed his act to balloon bending and his name to Windy Blow.

Felix the Cat

Heroes may come and heroes may go, but this one 'keeps on walking, keeps on walking still.' Pat Sullivan created him by chance one day, some say around 1919, for a small spot in *Feline Follies*, the closing segment of a magazine film entitled *The Paramount-Bray Pictograph.* Little more than a black blot with a tail (detachable, of course), Felix caught the film-goers' fancy and soon was a star. Promoted in song and strip, he was the first cartoon hero to know what real exploitation was. Not all his titles have been traced, but 78 were made between 1925 and 1929. His final film by Sullivan, who died in 1933, was appropriately entitled *The Last Life* (1929), but he made a comeback in colour in Burt Gillett's *Felix the Cat and the Goose that Laid the Golden Egg* (1936). He also came to life again for a new television series in the sixties. Felix is proving that a cartoon cat truly has nine lives!

"I'd go through fire and water for her-
but I'd sooner be nearer the fire!"

WORLD'S MOST FAMOUS CAT
HARVEY COMICS
APPROVED BY THE COMICS CODE AUTHORITY
Felix OCT. No. 100
10¢
PAT SULLIVAN'S
Felix the CAT
100TH ISSUE

Ferdinand

'He learned how to tango and dance the fandango, but he never learned how to fight.' So went the song that helped *Ferdinand the Bull* win a 1938 Academy Award for Walt Disney. This gentle creature who preferred blossomed meadows to bull rings, was adapted from the children's book *The Story of Ferdinand*, written by Munro Leaf and Robert Lawson.

Figaro

Pinocchio's pussy cat cut such cute kittenish capers with Cleo the goldfish in that famous 1940 feature, that Walt Disney extracted most of their original footage and allowed Jack Kinney to elaborate it into a complete short. *Figaro and Cleo* (1943) was followed by *Figaro and Frankie* (1946), with a new director in the shape of Charles Nichols.

Flebus

'A simple little character who wants everybody to like him', was how William Weiss, new vice-president of the reorganised *Terrytoons*, described the hero of *Flebus* (1957). This cinemascope short was the first of the 'New Look' cartoons produced by the ancient studio founded in New Rochelle by Paul Terry. Ernest Pintoff created Flebus and wrote the story in partnership with Gene Deitch, an ex-UPA cartoonist who became Creative Director of *Terrytoons*. Pintoff went on to make the better-known *Violinist* (1960).

Published by exclusive arrangement with

UB IWERKS,

The Originator of the Film Character, Flip the Frog.

Flip

Narrowly escaping being christened 'Tony Frog', Flip was the first cartoon hero created by Ub Iwerks, working outside the Disney studio, where he helped originate Mickey Mouse. Flip, who had a fine and funny theme song croaked to a honkytonk joanna, made his début in *Flying Fists* (1933) and starred in 12 films a year for three years before he finally croaked. One of Flip's animators was Stephen Bosustow, who years later founded the famed United Productions of America. All Flip's cartoons, which were made by Celebrity Productions for MGM release, were in black and white.

Flower

This sweet-smelling skunk was christened Flower by the baby Bambi in that famous feature film of Walt Disney's, made in 1942. Flower was a studio creation, and does not appear in the original novel by Felix Salten. Some may consider her as the 'mother' of Pepe Le Pew!

Foghorn Leghorn

Cock of the Warner Brothers walk ('Ah said walk!'), created by Bob McKimson, Foghorn won an Academy Award with his very first appearance, *Walky Talky Hawky* (1946). His characteristic double-talk, or rather double-up talk ('Ah said doubled-up talk!') stems from Southern Senator Claghorn, an American radio personality and is supplied by, of course, Mel Blanc. Latterday appearances include *Feather Bluster* (1958).

Friz Freleng

Winner of five Academy Awards (*Tweety Pie*, *Speedy Gonzales*, *Birds Anonymous*, *Knighty Knights Bugs*, *The Pink Phink*), Isadora Freleng, nicknamed Friz, was born in Kansas City. His first animation work was with Disney on *Oswald the Rabbit*; his first direction *Bosko in Dutch* (1932). Worked on Warner Brothers Looney Tunes/Merrie Melodies for 32 years before setting up DePatie-Freleng and producing Dr Seuss specials for television.

Foofoo

Foofoo 'the cheerful but displaced citizen', Gogo 'the rapacious villian', and the point of their eternal triangle, Mimi 'the overwhelming matron', starred in 31 black-and-white and two colour cartoons during 1959–60. Produced by John Halas and Joy Batchelor, they deserve a small niche in this history as the first British television cartoon heroes.

Fred Flintstone

Fred, head of the famous Flintstone household, left the television confines of prehistoric Bedrock for the wider spaces of the cinema in 1966. As *The Man Called Flintstone*, Fred found himself the double of Secret Agent Rock Slag. In this William Hanna–Joseph Barbera production, Fred was voiced as usual by Alan Reed, while the ubiquitous Mel Blanc was his buddy Barney Rubble.

Fox & Crow

Stars of a one-off in the Columbia series *Color Rhapsodies* entitled *The Fox and the Grapes* (1941) these two antagonists soon spun-off the one-off into a series of their own. Originally created by Frank Tashlin, their later mentors included Dave Fleischer, Bob Wickersham and John Hubley, who almost won them the Academy Award with *Robin Hoodlum* (1948). This *Jolly Frolics* entry was an early effort of the pace-setting production company UPA.

Fritz the Cat

That a cat should star in the first X-rated cartoon would make ancient Felix spin in his grave, were he not still walking! *Fritz the Cat* (1972), a 78-minute feature, was adapted by Ralph Bakshi from Robert Crumb's famous cat of the underground *Comix*, and given the voice of Skip Hinant. Robert Taylor directed the equally X-rated sequel, *The Nine Lives of Fritz the Cat* (1974).

Gabby

This tiny nightwatchman of Lilliput land stole *Gulliver's Travels* (1939) from under the very large nose of Gulliver himself. Gabby's song 'All's Well, It's A Rainy Day', was sung for him by Pinto Colvig. He was so popular that his creators, Max and Dave Fleischer, started him on his own in *Gabby Goes Fishing* (1941).

Gabby Gator

One of Woody Woodpecker's prime opponents in the Walter Lantz *Cartunes*, Gabby Gator, with his Southern-fried style of speech (Daws Butler) and his Southern-fried style of film *Southern Fried Hospitality* (1961), was created by Jack Hannah.

Gandy

Star of many a *Terrytoon*, Gandy was created by John Foster for *Gandy the Goose* (1938). Gandy's partner in crime and chase was Sourpuss the Cat. They were voiced from left to right by Arthur Kay and Tom Morrison, who kept them going for almost 20 years.

YES INDEED, PALS! SOURPUSS AND GANDY, AT YOUR SERVICE!
HE MEANS GANDY AND SOURPUSS, AT YOUR SERVICE!
I'M GONNA BE YOUR NEXT PIN-UP PICTURE-- SO **WATCH** FOR ME!

Gerald McBoing Boing

Reale name: Gerald McCloy. 'The strange thing that happened to that little boy' was that 'he couldn't say words, he said noises instead'. Dr Seuss (Theodore Geisel) created him in a book and John Hubley and Robert Cannon brought him to animated life at UPA, where his film, *Gerald McBoing-Boing* (1950) won the Academy Award. Marvin Miller as the story-teller. The Noise-making Boy appeared in several sequels: *Gerald McBoing-Boing's Symphony* (1953); the Cinemascope *How Now Boing Boing* (1954); and his own television series *The Gerald McBoing Boing Show*.

Gaston le Crayon

This would-be Lautrec, created by Gene Deitch for five of the new style *Terrytoons* under the aegis of the Columbia Broadcasting System, made his first appearance in the Cinemascope short *Gaston Is Here* (1957).

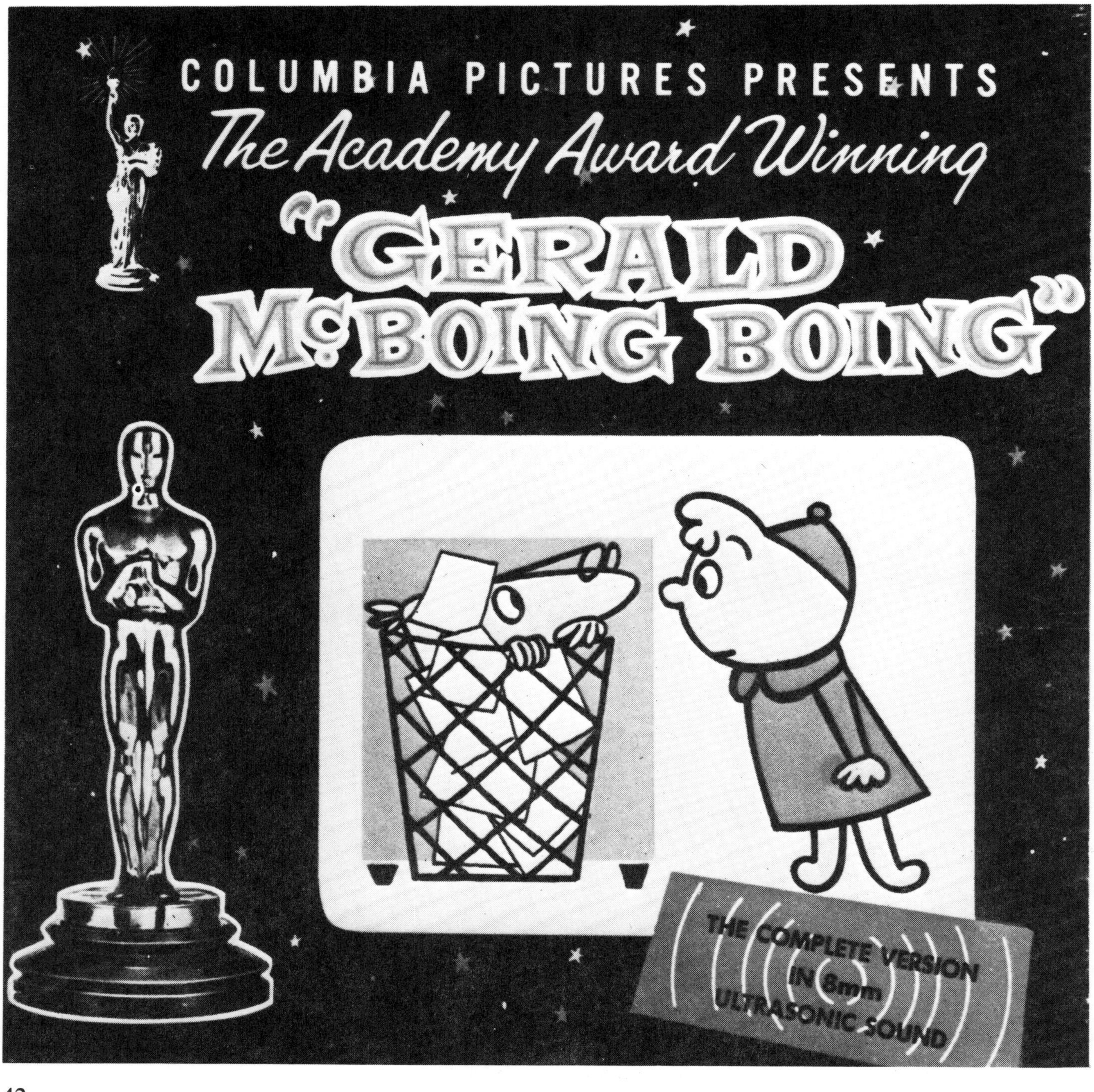

Gertie the Dinosaur

Legendary heroine of the 'first animated cartoon' according to many historians, there is, however, conflicting evidence as to the date of Gertie's first appearance. Winsor McCay, the famous comic strip artist of *Little Nero* who created her, may have hand-drawn a pilot version as early as 1909. However, his widely exhibited and extant film *Gertie the Trained Dinosaur*, was animated for him by John F. Bray in 1914. She appeared in a sequel, *Gertie On Tour*, some three years later.

Ginger & Hazel

The Nutts, Ginger and his sweetheart Hazel, were the first successful stars to emerge from David Hand's British-made *Animaland* series. First seen in *It's a Lovely Day* (1949), the two red squirrels reappeared later that year in *Ginger Nutt's Christmas Circus*, a grand and seasonable roundup of all the *Animaland* characters.

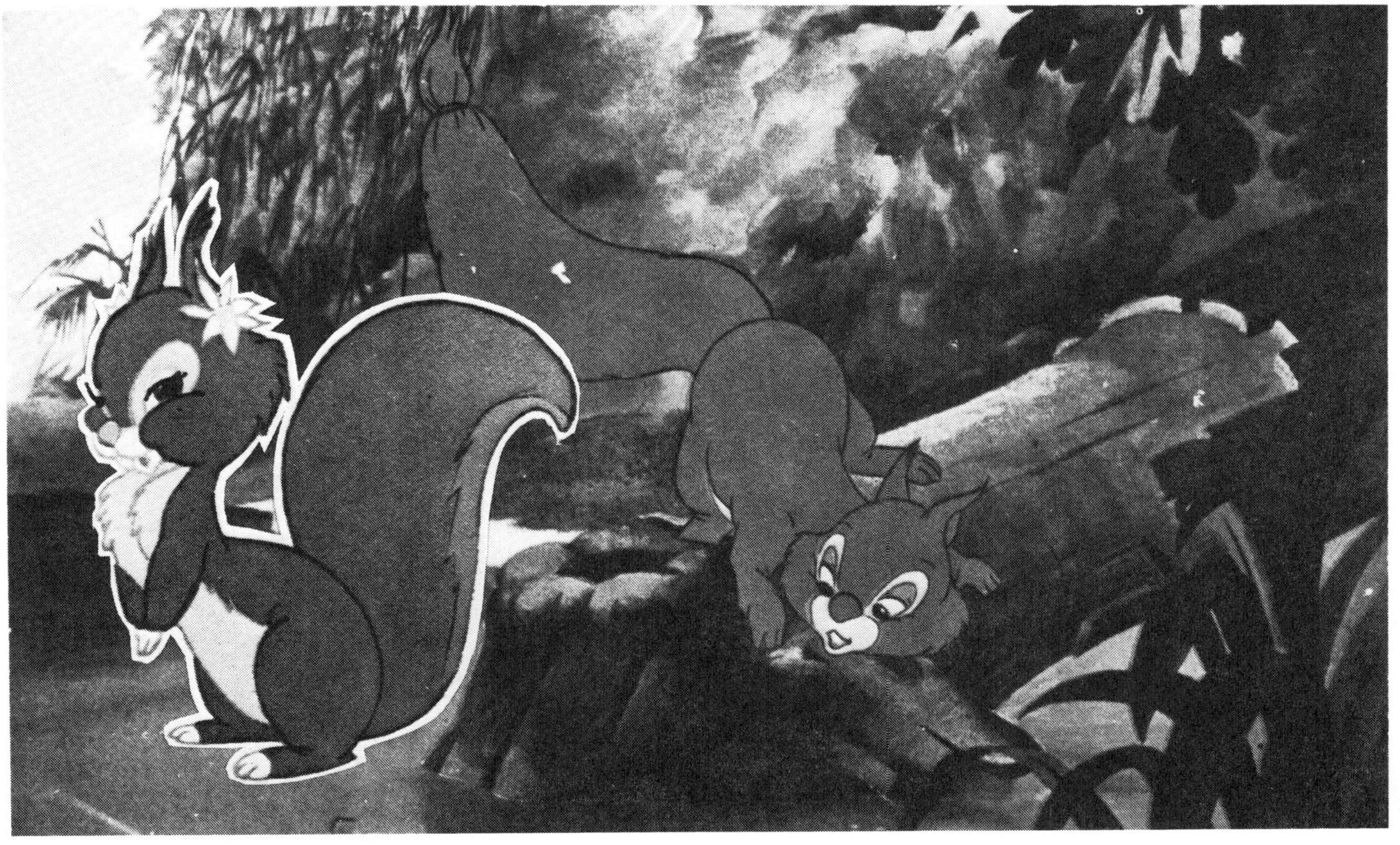

Goofy

Goofy's real name was Dippy Dawg. Once this bucktoothed hayseed changed his name to Goofy, he never looked back. Nor did he ever change his voice ('Gawrsh!'), which was ever that of Pinto Colvig. Goofy made his début in *Mickey's Revue* (1932), appeared in a number of threesome pictures (with Mickey and Donald Duck) like the classic *Clock Cleanears* (1937), and first shared top billing in *Goofy and Wilbur* (1939). In this Dick Huemer-directed short he shared screen-time with a grasshopper. Goofy's change of life came in the Walt Disney feature *The Reluctant Dragon* (1941), when he starred solo in the inserted short, *How to Ride a Horse*. This led to a long series of dippy documentaries starting with *The Art of Skiing* (1941) and ending with *How to Sleep* (1953).

George and Junior

Large (Junıor) and small (George) bears based on the large (Lennie) and small (George) humans in John Steinbeck's novel *Of Mice and Men*. Their voices, large (Tex Avery) and small (Frank Graham) make the movie parodies of Lon Chaney Jr and Burgess Meredith even neater. Among Tex Avery's funniest characters the made their debut in *Henpecked Hoboes* (1946).

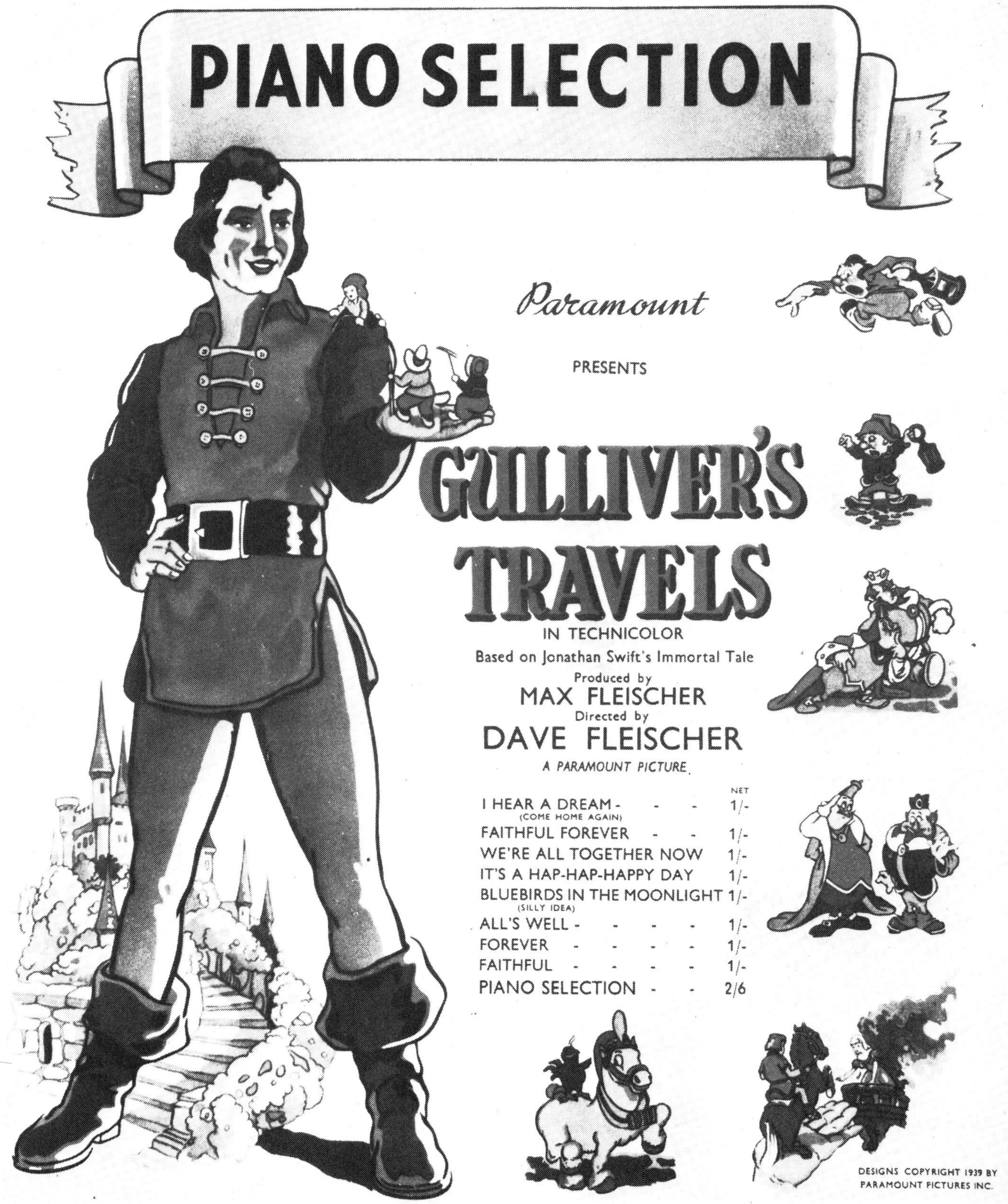

Gulliver

Lemuel Gulliver, created by Jonathan Swift in the book *Gulliver's Travels* (1726), was the shipwrecked sailor who settled the war between King Little and King Bombo, and who starred in the first feature-length cartoon in technicolour produced and directed by Max and Dave Fleischer (1939). Gulliver sang with the voice of Sam Brown: 'I Hear A Dream'.

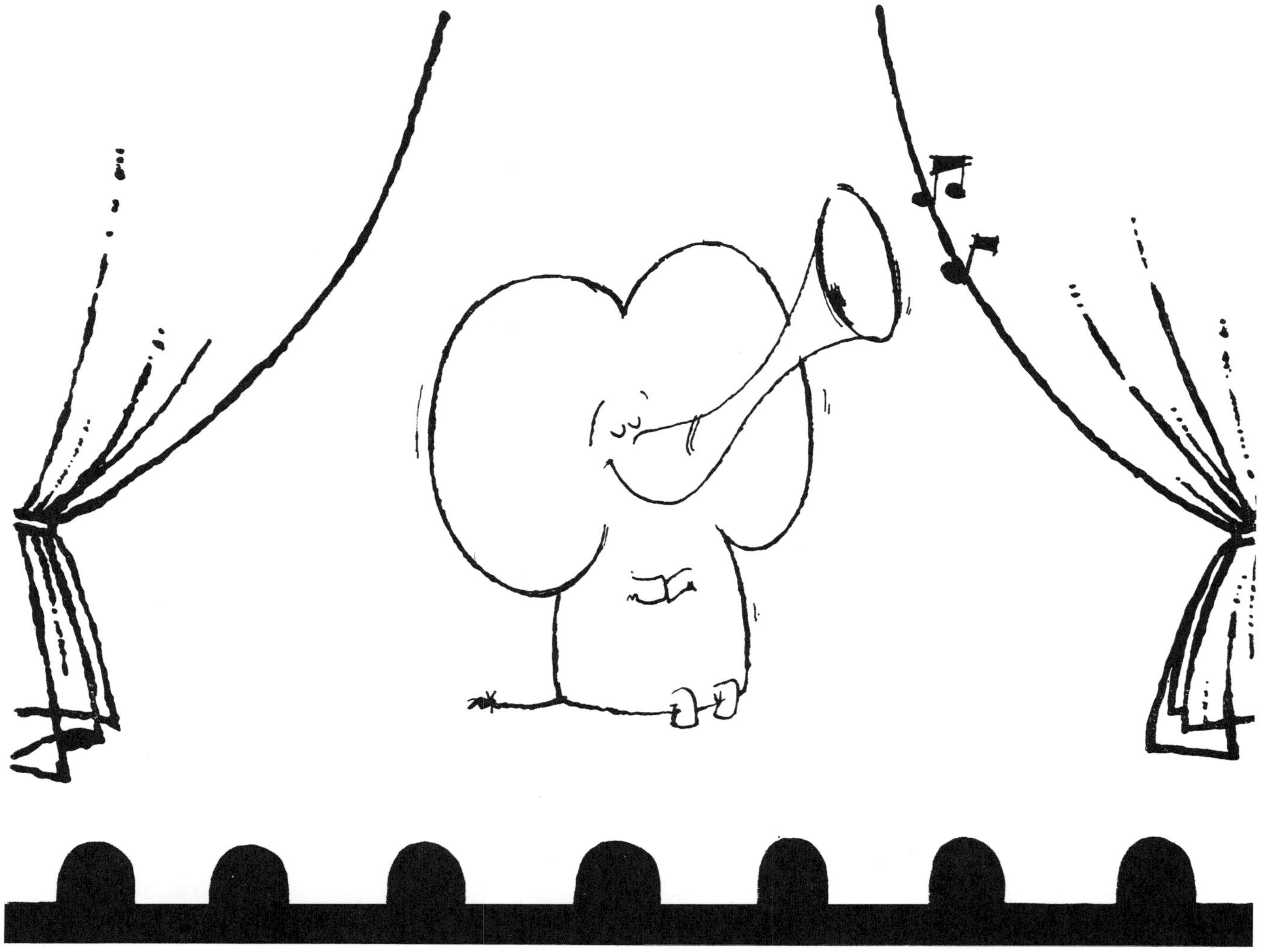

Gusgus & Jaq.

These two tiny little mice stole the show and saved the day in *Cinderella*, the 74-minute Walt Disney cartoon for 1950. A long way from Walt's Mickey, these mice were studio additions to the original fairy story by Charles Perrault. Jim MacDonald who spoke for both, gave them a marvellous mouse-lingo: 'Flinderelly, Flinderelly! Lookarook binju!' ('Cinderella, look behind you!').

Ham & Hattie

Although not related directly, Ham and Hattie were the inseparable stars of a double-barrelled series produced by UPA in 1958: their ultra-short shorts were released in pairs. The first release featured Hattie in *Trees*, and Hamilton Ham and his Band in *Jamaica Daddy*.

Happy Hooligan

The hobo with the tin-can hat was one one of the first American comic strip heroes. Happy Hooligan was created by Frederick Opper in 1899. Happy came to the animated screen in 1916 under the sponsorship of William Randolph Hearst. *He Tries the Movies Again*, was the first of 40 films made by Frank Moser, Ben Sharpsteen, Bill Nolan and the young Walt Lantz.

Heckle & Jeckle

Batty birds who first flew into view in *The Talking Magpies* (1946), which title quickly became their subtitle for a series. Heckle (or Jeckle) talks in the broadest of Brooklyn, while Jeckle (or Heckle) replies in the best of British accents. These voices were supplied by Tom Morrison and Dayton Allen. Heckle and Jeckle were created for *Terrytoons* by scriptwriter John Foster.

Hamilton

Heralded with much trumpeting for the studio's 21st birthday celebrations, *Hamilton the Musical Elephant* (1961) failed to spark off a series for Halas & Batchelor Cartoons. Hamilton's tuneful trunk was blown by bandleader/composer Johnny Dankworth.

Hashimoto

Last of a long line of animated mice, Hashimoto's honourable gimmick was that he was Japanese. Perhaps his director, Bob Kuwahara, was somehow to blame. A latterday *Terrytoon*, Hashimoto's voice was by the Hon. John Myhers. The first of his 12 cartoons was called *Hashimoto San* (1959).

Hector Heathcote

The Minute and a Half Man (1959) marked the début of half-pint hero Hector Heathcote. His six epic adventures in the days of the Colonial Wars broke new ground for both cartoons and *Terrytoons*. Hector was created by Dave Tendlar and spoken by John Myhers, while one of Hector's early animators was Ralph Bakshi, later the director of *Fritz the Cat*.

Henery Hawk

New-laid chicken hawk ever-determined to catch and eat a chicken, even if that chicken is kingsize rooster Foghorn Leghorn, Henery won an Oscar on his first outing: *Walky Talky Hawky* (1945). Henery's director: Bob McKimson. Henery's voice: Mel Blanc.

Herman and Katnip

Noveltoons' animated answer to MGM's Tom and Jerry, Herman the Mouse and Katnip the Cat came chasing out of *Naughty But Mice* (1947) and into their own full-blown series. Here director Seymour Kneitel let them enjoy such pun fun as *Of Mice and Menace* (1954). Their voices: Arnold Stang (Herman); and Syd Raymond (Katnip).

Hicks

Hicks was the henpecked hero of many an imaginative dream sequence. *Hicks in Nightmare Land* (1915) was a regular feature of *The Animated Grouch Chaser*, an early silent series released by the Thomas A. Edison company. Creator was the influential French animator Raoul Barré, one of the first cartoonists to set up a studio.

Homer Pigeon

One of the broodier breed of birds hatched by producer Walter Lantz in his Universal *Cartunes*, Homer Pigeon made his début in *Pigeon Patrol* (1942), directed by Alex Lovy. Created by Ben Hardaway, Homer later acquired a bird of his own called inevitably Carrie Pigeon.

Horton

Lisping pachyderm who meant what he said and said what he meant, 'cos an elephant's truthful one hundred per cent' in Dr Seuss's *Horton Hatches the Egg* (1942).

Horace Horsecollar

Stalwart of the original Mickey Mouse gang which scrambled all over the screen in such early Walt Disney shorts as *The Barn Dance* (1929), Horace's last major appearance was playing trombone in *The Band Concert* (1935), the first Mickey Mouse cartoon in technicolour.

Huey, Dewey & Louie

Donald Duck's naughty nephews made their first appearance in the aptly titled *Donald's Nephews* (1938), director Jack King. The triplets' voices were supplied by their Unca Donald's own Clarence Nash using a slightly higher key.

Hanna-Barbera

Mightiest of modern cartoon companies, the combination of William Hanna (born Melrose 1920) and Joseph Barbera (born New York 1911) began officially in 1940 with *Gallopin' Gals*, and continued through *Tom and Jerry* into such television series as *Huckleberry Hound*. Oscars: *Yankee Doodle Mouse* (1943), *Mouse Trouble* (1944), *Quiet Please* (1945), *Cat Concerto* (1946), *Little Orphan* (1948), *Two Mouseketeers* (1951), *Johann Mouse* (1952).

Hoffnung

Cartoonist Gerard Hoffnung's little books of musical cartoons were animated into a series of technicolor shorts by John Halas and Joy Batchelor. The first, *The Hoffnung Symphony Orchestra* (1965), won several awards.

ALL NEW
Hanna-Barbera
PARADE
HARLTON
COMICS
0765·1272
BY THE COMICS CODE AUTHORITY
ONLY 20¢
NO. 10
DEC.
CDC

Inki

African infant who doggedly pursues (but never catches) the mystic Mynah Bird, a curious creature who hops to the tune of Mendelssohn's 'Fingal's Cave'. Created by Chuck Jones for *Little Lion Hunter* (1939), the pursuit plodded on for a decade, ending with *Caveman Inki* (1950).

Ichabod Crane

The sonorously named Ichabod is the scared schoolmaster of Sleepy Hollow who loses Katrina Van Tassel to Brom Bones when the latter dolls up as the Headless Horseman. Created by humorous writer Washington Irving in 1819, this pillar of small-town society was filmed by Walt Disney in 1949 as the second half of the 68-minute feature, *Ichabod and Mr Toad. The Legend of Sleepy Hollow* was told and sung by Bing Crosby, and Ben Sharpsteen was production supervisor.

Inspector Willoughby

Determined if not dogged detective, reminiscent of a humanised Droopy, he first appeared as Ranger Willoughby of Peachstone National Park in *Hunger Strife* and as Truant Officer Willoughby in *Truant Student* before settling down with Scotland Yard. The Inspector is named after Willoughby Avenue, where stands Walter Lantz and his *Cartune* Studio, and is best remembered as the bold apprehender of Yeggs Benedict in *The Case of the Cold Storage Yegg* (1962), directed by Paul J. Smith. His voice is that of Dal McKennon.

Inspector Clouseau

Inspector Jacques Clouseau, accident-prone plainclothes man from the Paris Sûreté, first appeared on film in *A Shot in the Dark* (1964) as portrayed by Peter Sellers. Animated opening titles were created for the picture by De Patie/Freleng, who then developed the character into a cartoon in its own right. Echoes of Sellers are heard in the words spoken by Pat Harrington Jr., in *French Freud* (1968) and the rest of the Inspector's cartoon cases.

J. Wellington Wimpy

Hamburger-munching moocher and stolid supporter of Popeye the Sailor Man, in spirit if not in muscle ('Let's you and him fight!'), Mr Wimpy was created by E. C. Segar in his *Thimble Theatre* comic strip, in memory of a grandiloquent referee at the Santa Monica Ocean Park Arena. Wimpy appeared in several of the Max Fleischer *Popeye* cartoons for Paramount with a voice provided by Frank Matalone.

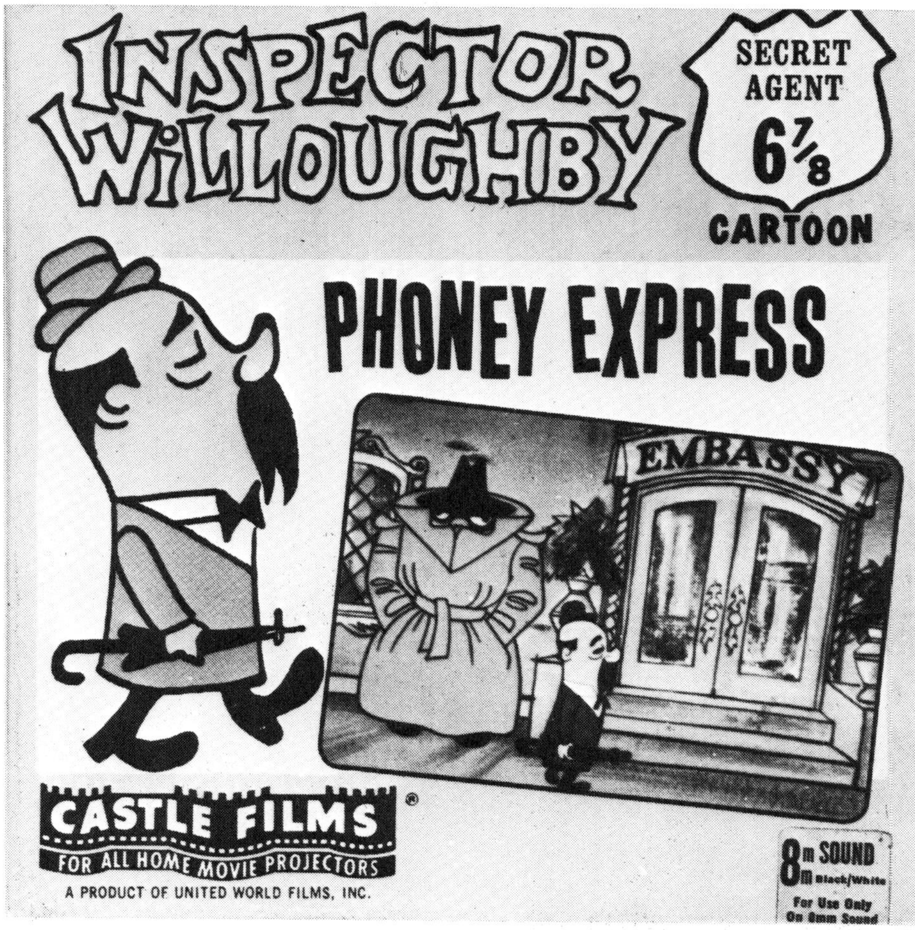
INSPECTOR WILLOUGHBY
SECRET AGENT 6 7/8
CARTOON
PHONEY EXPRESS
EMBASSY
CASTLE FILMS
FOR ALL HOME MOVIE PROJECTORS
A PRODUCT OF UNITED WORLD FILMS, INC.
SOUND
Black/White
For Use Only
On 8mm Sound

J Worthington Foul Fellow

Known as 'Honest John' to his cronies in crime, notably Gideon his side-kick cat, this sly fox led Pinocchio the puppet boy astray with his song of freedom, 'Hi Diddle Dee Dee, An Actor's Life For Me'. The Hollywood character comedian Walter Catlett both posed and spoke for Honest John in Walt Disney's *Pinocchio* (1940).

Jolly Frolics

Series title for the early Stephen Bosustow UPA cartoons made for Columbia, from which sprang such stars as Mr Magoo and Gerald McBoing Boing.

Jerky Journeys

Four unlikely travelogue burlesques produced by Impossible Pictures Inc in Trucolor. Written and directed by Leonard Louis Levinson and narrated by radio comedian Frank Nelson in his character of 'Senator Claghorn'. The only cartoons distributed by Republic Pictures.

Jiminy Cricket

The eighteen carat Official Conscience of Pinocchio the puppet in the 1940 Walt Disney feature of the same name. Jiminy was spoken and, especially, sung by Cliff 'Ukelele Ike' Edwards: 'When You Wish Upon a Star' and 'Give a Little Whistle' by Leigh Harline, Ned Washington, and Paul Smith. Jiminy reappeared as link man for *Fun and Fancy Free* (1947), a duty he continues on Disney television shows.

Joe Carioca

Joe Carioca was the brolly-bandishing Brazilian bird who taught Donald Duck to samba in *Saludos Amigos* (1943), Walt Disney's response to President Roosevelt's Good Neighbor Policy. Joe pops up again in *The Three Caballeros* (1945) singing 'Baia' in the voice of Aloysio (Jose) Oliveira.

John Doormat

Norman Ferguson directed both films. John and the formidable Mrs Doormat starred in four Cinemascope cartoons, beginning with *Topsy T.V.* (1957). 'A sort of Mr America fellow who is highly fad conscious' was how William Weiss, the man who took over *Terrytoons*, described this hen-pecked hero created by Gene Deitch. Spoken for, if not up for, by Bern Bennett.

Joys'n'Glooms

These little characters who lurk in the corners of newspaper cartoons drawn by Tom Powers were brought to life by Raoul Barré in his 1916 series *Funnygraphs*, produced by Press Baron William Randolph Hearst.

Julius

Black cat, suspiciously similar to Felix, who was the cartoon companion to the live action Virginia Davis in *Alice in Cartoonland*, Walt Disney's first series made for Winkler Pictures 1924–1926.

Katzenjammer Kids

Hans and (pardon, 'und') Fritz Katzenjammer – by name and nature, Katzenjammer means 'hangover' – exploded in American newspaper comics as early as 1897. Rudolph Dirks created them, and Gregory La Cava and George Stallings animated them. They made their début with their seafaring stepfather (2) in *Der Captain Goes Swimming* (1916).

Koko the Clown

Out of the Inkwell he came one day, and he came to stay. From that early series (1918) in which he co-starred with his live-action creator, Max Fleischer, Koko continued his ink-redible capers right through the Betty Boop cartoons of the thirties, to TV's *Out of the Inkwell* in the sixties. Farewell appearance: *Koko Meets Barney Beatnik* (1963) at the ripe old age of 55.

Kiko the Kangaroo

This boxing kangaroo hopped into *Terrytoons* as Paul Terry's cartoon contender for 1936. He lasted but six rounds, despite stalwart support from Farmer Gray (Al Falfa). *Kiko and the Honey Bears* was the first entry, directed by Mannie Davis.

Krazy Kat

The Kraziest Kat in Komics Komes to Kartoons. Of the many honours heaped upon George Herriman's hero (heroine?) from the funny papers, that of being the first cartoon cat is the least mentioned. *Introducing Krazy Kat and Ignatz Mouse* (1916), animated by Frank Moser, began a career that continued with Winkler (Bill Nolan's *Chicken Chaser*, 1926), went into sound at Columbia (Harrison & Gould's *Canned Music* 1930), and ended with *Little Lost Sheep* (1939) by which time he/she/it was a long way from Kokonino Kounty.

KRAZY KAT AND IGNATZ MOUSE GO INTO THE MOVIES

ANC
LITTLE
ROQUEFORT
COMICS
ST. JOHN
TRADEMARK
No. 9
TEN CENTS
TOOTHPASTE
HOUSEHOLD
CEMENT

Keeping Up with the Joneses

Famous newspaper strip by Arthur 'Pop' Momand, animated for the Gaumont Company by another newspaper strip cartoonist, Harry Palmer. The first, *Dancing Lessons*, was released in 1915, and featured the regular characters Pa and Ma McGinnis.

Lambert

This was the lion who lay down with the lamb, because he thought he was one. The identity crisis occurred in *Lambert the Sheepish Lion* (1952), directed by Jack Hannah and nominated for the Academy Award.

Little Audrey

The little girl who laughed and laughed and laughed: or at any rate, she did in those Little Audrey stories that were all the rage in the thirties. Created by Larz Bourne, the animated Audrey starred in a *Noveltoon* series directed by Seymour Kneitel. The first one was called *Santa's Surprise* (1947).

Lady & the Tramp

The pedigree pup who fell in love with a mongrel from the wrong side of the tracks was the heroine of Ward Greene's story, *Lady and the Tramp*. Walt Disney made the 75-minute film version in 1955, and gave her the voice of Barbara Luddy. Tramp's voice was Larry Roberts and Peggy Lee sang their song. The film was directed by Hamilton Luske, Clyde Geronimi and Wilfred Jackson.

Little Roquefort

He was one of *Terrytoons*' answers to Tom and Jerry. Little Roquefort (mouse) was chased by Percy (cat) through a good many (but not many good) films written by John Foster, directed by Mannie Davis, and voiced by Tom Morrison. Early entry: *Cat Happy* (1950).

Lil Abner

Scion of the Yokum family of Dogpatch, U.S. of A., Al Capp's hillbilly hero from the Sunday supplements was animated for Columbia cartoons by producer Dave Fleischer and director Bob Wickersham. He appeared in four shorts only, despite a head start with *Sadie Hawkins' Day* (1944).

Little Cheeser

The cute li'l mouse's name was a pun on Edward G. Robinson's *Little Caesar*. Cheeser parodied another contemporary hero, Buck Rogers, in *Little Buck Cheeser* (1937), a Hugh Harman-Rudolph Ising *Happy Harmonies* cartoon for MGM.

Lil Eightball

Hapless if not shiftless, this piccaninny hit hard luck in several Walter Lantz *Cartunes* for Universal, starting with *The Stubborn Mule* (1939).

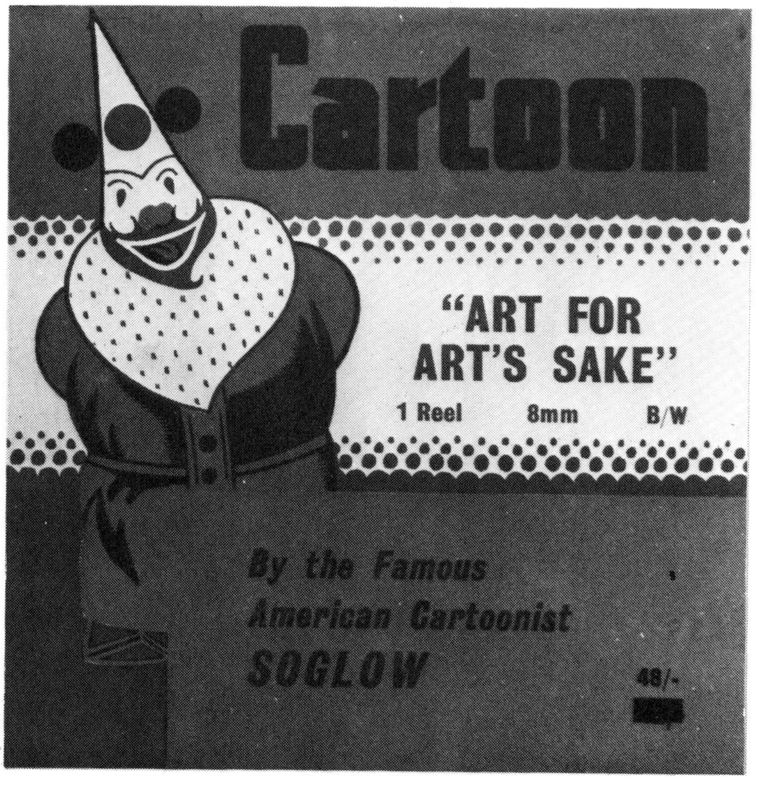

Little King

Silent star of the Sunday Funnies where he was created by Otto Soglow, he starred in 10 Van Bueren cartoons for director George Stallings. The first was called *The Fatal Note* (1933). Later he guest-starred in Max Fleischer's *Betty Boop and the Little King* (1936).

Little Lulu

Angelic innocent ever up to pantomime mischief, Little Lulu started her cartoon career in the *Saturday Evening Post* of 23 February 1935. She was the creation of lady cartoonist Marge (Marjorie Henderson Buell). Isidore Sparber brought Lulu to Famous Studios for a Paramount series beginning with *Eggs Don't Bounce* (1943), written by Carl Meyer, Jack Mercer and Jack Ward.

Looney Tunes

Series produced by Leon Schlesinger for Warner Brothers, beginning with the black and white *Singin' in the Bathtub* (1930), starring Bosko. Early series stars: Buddy, Porky Pig, Daffy Duck.

Mad Hatter

'A Very Merry Unbirthday To You' sang the Mad Hatter to Alice in the cracked voice of oldtime comic Ed Wynn. The Hatter's Mad Tea Party was a highlight of Walt Disney's *Alice in Wonderland* (1951), a sequence directed by Ward Kimball. Just as Mad as the Hatter, if not madder, the March Hare was blessed with the unlikely larynx of mad musician Jerry Colonna in Walt Disney's *Alice in Wonderland* (1951).

March Hare

He more than managed to avoid comparison with that well-established wild hare, Bugs Bunny.

Loopy de Loop

Ze good wolf who only does ze good deeds, but alas! Loopy was the misunderstood hero of William Hanna and Joseph Barbera's attempt to return to the cinema screen after some time with television. *Tale of a Wolf* (1959) was first. Voice: Daws Butler.

Loopy Hare

He provided spring-heeled character support in David Hand's *Animaland* cartoons, a British series too short-lived to allow the likely Loopy to develop. He made his début in *It's a Lovely Day* (1949).

Madam Mim

Another self-confessed lunatic ('Mad Madam Mim' sang Madam Mim, the wicked witch), she worked her wiles in *The Sword in the Stone* (1963), wrenched by Walt Disney from the classic novel of T. H. White. When Merlin the Magician changed Wart (young King Arthur) to a bird, Madam Mim changed herself to a rat! Her evil voice was Martha Wentworth's.

Little Cesario

Although his name is a pun on Edward G. Robinson's *Little Caesar*, Little Cesario is as unlike that gangster movie as can be. He is the try-and-try-again little pup of Rudolf Ising's 1941 epic of snowbound St Bernards.

Maud the Mule

High-kicking heroine of Frederick Burr Opper's ancient comic page, *And Her Name Was Maud*, she cantered into cartoons in 1916 for *A Quiet Day in the Country*. Gregory La Cava supervised this William Randolph Hearst production.

Merlin

The wizened but with-it wizard of *The Sword in the Stone* (1963), featured in Walt Disney's production of Bill Peet's adaptation of T. H. White's novel. In his education of Wart, the once and future King, Merlin (voice: Karl Swenson) defeats Madam Mim in a duel of magic. The film was directed by Wolfgang Reitherman.

Merrie Melodies

Secondary series title for the Leon Schlesinger cartoons produced for Warner Brothers. Originally rooted in songs from the parent company's musicals, such as *I Only Have Eyes for You* (1933), stars such as Porgy Pig, Daffy Duck and Bugs Bunny were later introduced.

Max Hare

Max was the smarty star of *The Tortoise and the Hare*, the Walt Disney *Silly Symphony* which won the Academy Award for 1934. Max didn't beat Toby Tortoise to the post, but his hare-brained hiphops undoubtedly inspired the Warner Brothers' Bugs Bunny. Director: Wilfred Jackson.

Mewsette

This provincial feline left her native Provence for suave Meowrice and *Gay Purr-ee* (1962), but was saved from catastrophe by her country lover, Jaune Tom. This 58-minute feature from United Productions of America was written by Chuck Jones, directed by Abe Levitow, and purred ('Paris Is A Lonely Town') by Judy Garland.

Max Fleischer

Second only to Walt Disney in the history of American animation, Max Fleischer (1889–1972), with his younger brother Dave as director, animated and produced cartoons from 1917. His first major series *Out of the Inkwell* starring Koko the Clown blended live action and animation, and led to the invention of the rotoscope, a device still in constant use. Top series: *Betty Boop* and *Popeye*. Features: *Gulliver's Travels* (1939), *Mr Bug Goes to Town* (1942).

Leon Schlesinger
PRODUCES
LOONEY TUNES
AND
MERRIE MELODIES
FOR WARNER BROS. RELEASE
PORKY
LEON SCHLESINGER PRODUCTIONS
WARNER BROS. STUDIO HOLLYWOOD

THE VOICE OF
JUDY GARLAND

Mickey Mouse

With his disc-black ears, his sliced-pie eyes, his three-stripe gloves and his red-buttoned pants, Mickey (almost Mortimer) Mouse towers over the talkie cartoon, having thoroughly usurped the crown of Felix the Cat, his rival from the silent era. Created by Walt Disney, developed by Ub Iwerks, Mickey's delayed début was in *Plane Crazy* (1928): delayed because his third film, *Steamboat Willie* (1928) was shown first! With a mouth-organ soundtrack blown by animator Wilfred Jackson, Mickey quickly jigged his way to international stardom to the tune of 'Turkey In The Straw'. Mickey's first words were spoken by Carl Stalling, 'Oh shucks, that's nothin'!' in *Wild Waves* (1929). Disney himself took on the vocal chores until 1935, then it's James MacDonald who whistles and calls 'Hey, Pluto!'. Mickey's feature film appearances: *Fantasia* (1940); *Fun and Fancy Free* (1947). Mr Michael Mouse left the screen in 1953 after *The Simple Things*, and now lives in pleasant retirement at Uncle Walt's fun empire, Disneyland.

Minnie Mouse

Heroine of more than her fair share of Mickey Mouse movies without ever once receiving star billing, Miss (never a Mrs) Mouse was a Walt Disney contract player right from her first film, which was *Plane Crazy* (1928), directed by Ub Iwerks. Minnie's voice was first provided by Marcellite Garner in *Cactus Kid* (1930): 'My hero!' she squeaked abjectly.

Miranda Panda

Mickey Mouse has his Minnie, Homer Pigeon his Carrie, so naturally Andy Panda has his Miranda. A Walter Lantz *Cartune* creation, her appearances seem more frequent in the comicbooks than the movies.

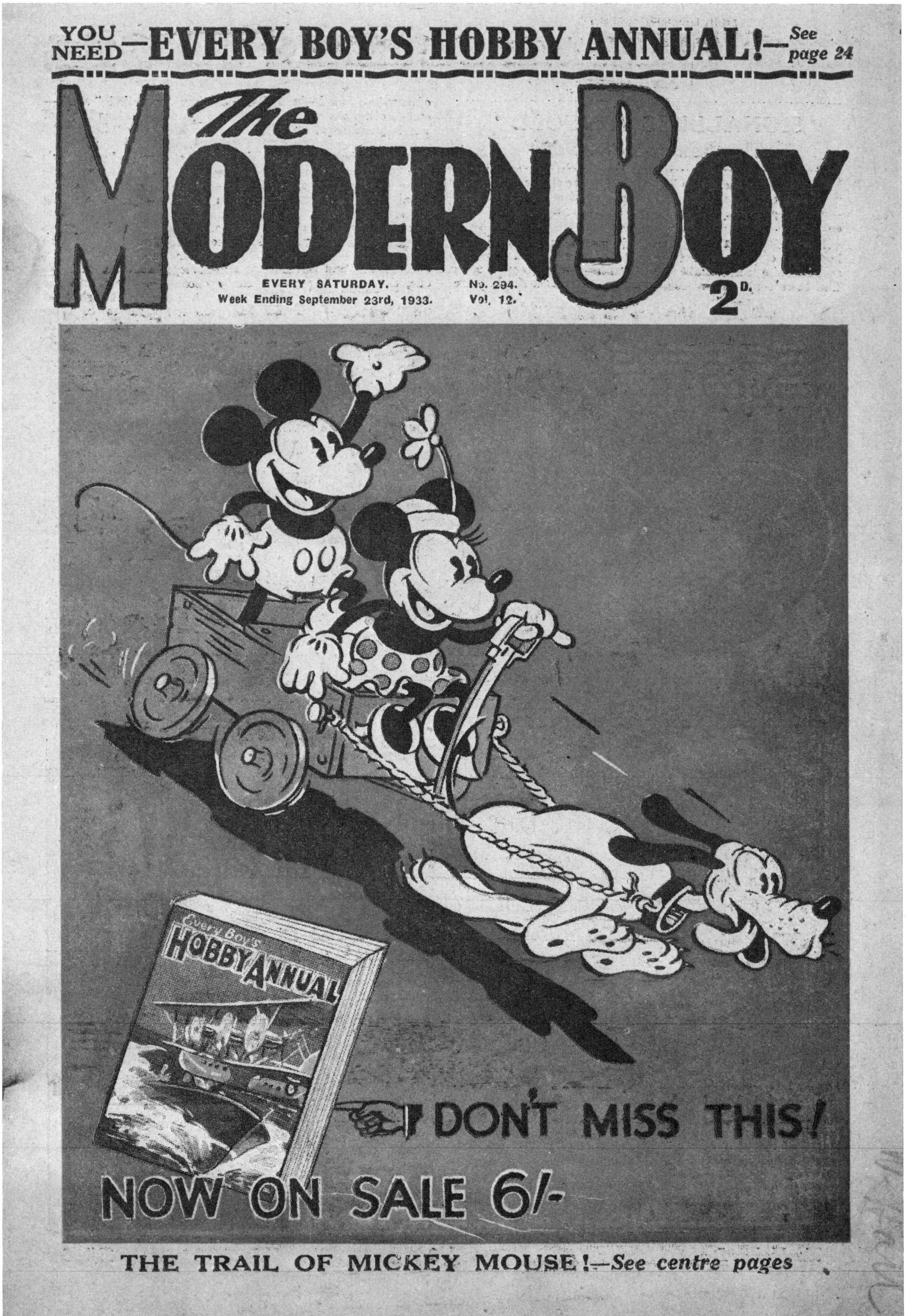
YOU NEED—EVERY BOY'S HOBBY ANNUAL!—See page 24
The MODERN BOY
EVERY SATURDAY.
Week Ending September 23rd, 1933.
No. 294.
Vol. 12.
2D.
Every Boy's HOBBY ANNUAL
DON'T MISS THIS!
NOW ON SALE 6/-
THE TRAIL OF MICKEY MOUSE!—See centre pages

Mighty Mouse

Who will save the mice of the world when the cats come calling? Why, none other than Mighty Mouse! This champion of the oppressed rodents packs more punch than the average *Terrytoon* hero, but was unable to defeat the mighty National Comics empire when they demanded he change his original name from Super Mouse! First seen in *Super Mouse in Pandora's Box* (1943), he sported his new name in *Mighty Mouse Meets Jekyll and Hyde Cat* (1944). Created by John Foster, he sings with the voice of Roy Halee.

Mr Bug

Mr Bug was the titular hero of Max Fleischer's second feature-length production, *Mr Bug Goes to Town* (1941). Paramount's British end changed the name to *Hoppity Goes to Town*, thus sacrificing humour for clarity. (The original title parodied *Mr Deeds Goes to Town.*) Hoppity the grasshopper who led his beloved Honey Bee and the other bugs to a new, safer life in a garden atop a skyscraper, was created by Dave Fleischer, Dan Gordon, Ted Pierce and Isidore Sparber. He sang songs by Hoagy Carmichael, Frank Loesser and Sammy Timberg.

Mr Magoo

Near-sighted hero, despite himself, of the UPA *Jolly Frolics* cartoon, *Ragtime Bear* (1949), Mr Magoo subsequently stumbled and bumbled his myopic way through 52 shorts and a 76-minute feature film, *1001 Arabian Nights* (1959). He won the Academy Award for *When Magoo Flew* (1955) and *Magoo's Puddle Jumper* (1956) in Cinemascope. Spoken, if that is the word, by Jim Backus; created, and that *is* the word, by John Hubley and Millard Kaufman.

Mr Stork

The straw-haired delivery boy causes a little confusion in Walt Disney's *Dumbo* (1941) and more in *Lambert the Sheepish Lion* (1951). Spoken by, and looking remarkably like, the film actor Sterling Holloway.

J. Thaddeus Toad, Squire of Toad Hall and noted motor lover, tooted out of Kenneth Grahame's whimsical

Mr Toad

Wind in the Willows (1908) and hooted into Walt Disney's *Ichabod and Mr Toad* (1949). This feature, produced by Ben Sharpsteen, was directed by Jack Kinney, Clyde Geronimi and James Algar. Toad's tale was told by Basil Rathbone, his voice was croaked by Eric Blore. Toad was reissued in 1967 as a 73-minute featurette under the original title of the book, still singing 'Merrily On Our Way'.

Miss Nanny Goat

Miss Nanny Goat Becomes an Aviator was the title of the first of a short series of cartoons created by newspaper strip artist Clarence Rigby. It was released in 1916 by the Bray Studios.

Mowgli

This orphaned Indian mancub was raised in the jungle by a pair of wolves and befriended by Bagheera the panther and Baloo the bear. In return, Mowgli saves his animal pals from Shere Khan the tiger. Created by Rudyard Kipling in 1894 and filmed in 1967 as the 78-minute *Jungle Book*, it was the last personal production by Walt Disney. Mowgli's voice was dubbed by young Bruce Reitherman, son of the film's director Wolfgang.

Mutt & Jeff

Mutt, short for A. Mutt, and Jeff, short for Jeffries, first met in a Booby Hatch drawn by Bud Fisher in 1909. Their daily newspaper strip was such a success that Bud Fisher formed Mutt and Jeff Films in 1916. His first animated release was *Jeff's Toothache*. Raoul Barré directed with Isadore Klein and Seymour Kneitel animating. Fox Films took over distribution and the double act made a weekly appearance for some years. Revived in 1925 by Associated Animators, a cooperative of cartoonists including Dick Huemer and Burt Gillett, Mutt and Jeff failed to make it into the talkie era.

Mr Fuller Pep

Enthusiastic and well meaning, this breezy character made his debut in *Mr Fuller Pep, He Tries Mesmerism* (1916). Created by F. M. Follett for Powers Films, Pep ran to nine adventures.

F.B.O. Mutt and Jeff Cartoons are the Pick of the Batch.

Napoleon

'All Animals Are Equal' proclaimed Napoleon, leader of the revolution that ejected Farmer Jones from *Animal Farm* (1954). 'But some are more equal than others,' he added, making himself Dictator. John Halas and Joy Batchelor produced this first British cartoon feature (72 minutes) for Louis de Rochemont. It was adapted from George Orwell's notable novel, and Maurice Denham did Napoleon's voice – and everybody else's!

Old Doc Yak

This old goat butted into the business by way of the funny papers. Sidney Smith drew Doc's comic strip, then animated him for 17 films via Selig Polyscope, finally producing him as a tailpiece for *The Chicago Tribune Animated Weekly*, a 1913 newsreel.

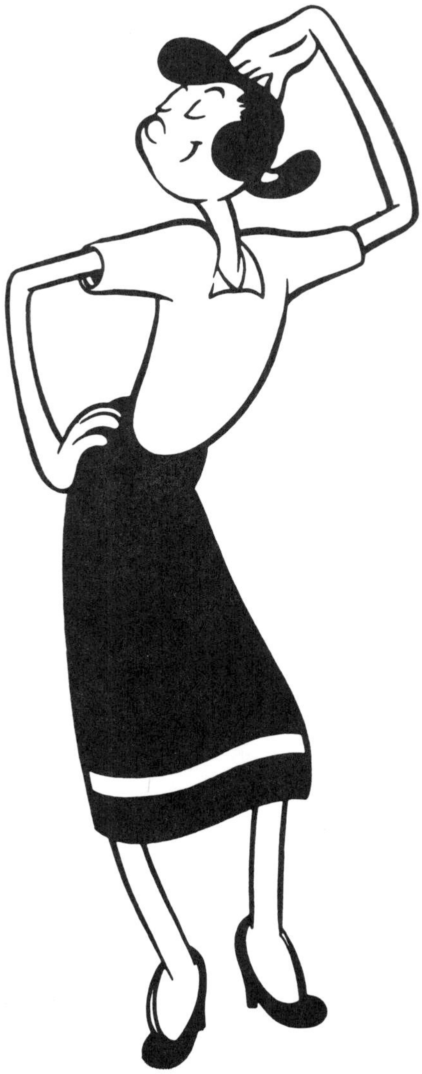

One Hundred and One Dalmations

Pongo (Rod Taylor's voice) and Perdita (Cate Bauer) plus 99 puppies add up to the *101 Dalmations* in the title of this 79-minute Walt Disney feature from 1961. Adapted by Bill Peet from Dodie Smith's novel, the dogs literally blotted their spotted copybook: they were animated by Xerox! They had three directors: Wolfgang Reitherman, Hamilton Luske and Clyde Geronimi.

Olive Oyl

Lath-legged lady heroine of the *Thimble Theatre* comic strip created in 1919 by E. C. Segar, Olive Oyl came to the screen in 1933 as the ham in the Popeye/Bluto sandwich. Producer: Max Fleischer. Voice: Mae Questal. Brother: Castor Oyl.

'Orace the 'Ound

'Orace the 'Armonious 'Ound was the star of the first sound cartoon made in Britain. Animated and produced at the Wembley Studios by Joe Noble and his brother George, 'Orace appeared in a burlesque of Al Jolson entitled *The Jazz Stringer* (1929).

Oswald the Rabbit

Subtitled *The Lucky Rabbit*, this little black character did not prove so for his cartoonist creators, Walt Disney and Ub Iwerks. But come up lucky he did for Hugh Harman and Rudolph Ising, who took Oswald over in 1928 (animator Friz Freleng). He proved even more lucky for Walter Lantz, who took him over in turn, whitewashing him in 1930 (animator Tex Avery). Oswald's Disney début: *Trolley Troubles* (1927). Oswald's talkie voice: Bernice Hansen, with some early help from Mickey Rooney!

Pablo

The original cold-blooded penguin, whatever Chilly Willy might claim, Pablo and his hot-water bottle appeared under the classification *Aves Raras* (strange birds) in Walt Disney's 1945 feature *The Three Caballeros*. Pablo's tale was told by Sterling Holloway. Director: Clyde Geronimi.

Panchito

One of the 'three happy chappies in snappy serapes' who made up *The Three Caballeros* (1945), Walt Disney's second jaunt south of the border. The other two were Donald Duck and Joe Carioca. A Mexican charro rooster by trade, Panchito tells his guests about the local Christmas traditions.

DELL
10¢
MAGAZINE
No. 143
OSWALD
the RABBIT
and the
PREHISTORIC
EGG

Paul Terry

Paul H. Terry (1888–1972), father of the *Terrytoons*, was a newspaper cartoonist who entered animation by making *Little Herman* (1915). His first star was *Farmer Al Falfa* who starred in *Down on Phoney Farm* (1915), followed by *Aesop's Fables* from 1920, and *Terrytoons* from 1930. On the occasion of his 1,000th cartoon, *Flatfoot Fledgling*, a retrospective was held at the Museum of Modern Art, New York. Terry was one of the first to economise in the number of drawings neccessary to produce movement, reducing the average for a reel cartoon from 20,000 to 3,500.

Pecos Bill

'He was the toughest critter west of the Alamo'. – so testified the Sons of the Pioneers of Pecos Bill. Roy Rogers the king of the cowboys himself, told Bill's tall tale in *Melody Time* (1948), a Walt Disney cartoon revue, and little Bobby Driscoll believed every word of how Bill's jealous boss Widowmaker bounced Sluefoot Sue to the moon. Director: Jack Kinney.

Peg leg Pete

The dirtiest villain in cartoons, Bluto included, Mickey Mouse regularly put paid to Pete from *Gallopin' Gaucho* (1929) on. Later his kindly creator, Walt Disney, let Pete grow another leg! Pete's voice: Billy Bletcher.

Peter and the Wolf

Brave young Russian hunter who,

Bird and Sonja the Duck, tracks down the wild Wolf in the 'Fairy Tale with Music' chapter of Disney's *Make Mine Music* (1946). Told by Sterling Holloway to the music of Serge Prokoviev.

PAUL TERRY'S
COMICS
No. 100 TEN CENTS
TERRY-TOONS
MIGHTY MOUSE
HECKLE AND JECKLE
GANDY GOOSE
ART OF BOW AND ARROW

Pepe le Pew

Monsieur Le Pew puts on more airs than Charles Boyer; he's a skunk! But an amorous one, and Pepe intends no more than love and kisses whatever his pathetic victims might scent. Created by Chuck Jones, Pepe won the Academy Award on his first outing, *For Scenti-Mental Reasons* (1949). He was another Warner Brothers *Looney Tunes* character voiced by the incredible Mel Blanc.

Peter Pan

Titular star of *Peter Pan* (1953) and leader of the Lost Children, Peter Pan finds time to teach Wendy Darling to fly with the aid of Tinker Bell's Pixie Dust, and duly saves her from the clutches of piratical Captain Hook. Peter was created by Sir James M. Barrie in his 1904 play, filmed by Walt Disney in 1953, modelled by dancer Roland Dupree, and given a voice by Bobby Driscoll.

Pink Panther

The coolest cat in cartoons was created by David De Patie and Friz Freleng for the opening credits of Blake Edwards' film *The Pink Panther* (1964). His first spin-off solo, *Pink Phink* (1964), won the Academy Award. By 1972, he had starred in 71 shorts, the record for a modern-day cartoon star. P.P.'s first director and writer were respectively, Hawley Pratt and John Dunn.

Pat Sullivan

Patrick Sullivan (1887–1933) was the most famous animator of the silent cartoon film period. His first series featured the hero of his own newspaper strip, *Sammie Johnsin* (1916). Later came *Charlie* (1918) and *Hardrock Dome* (1919), but all were excelled by his creation of the first cartoon hero to archieve world-wide acclaim, *Felix the Cat* (1920).

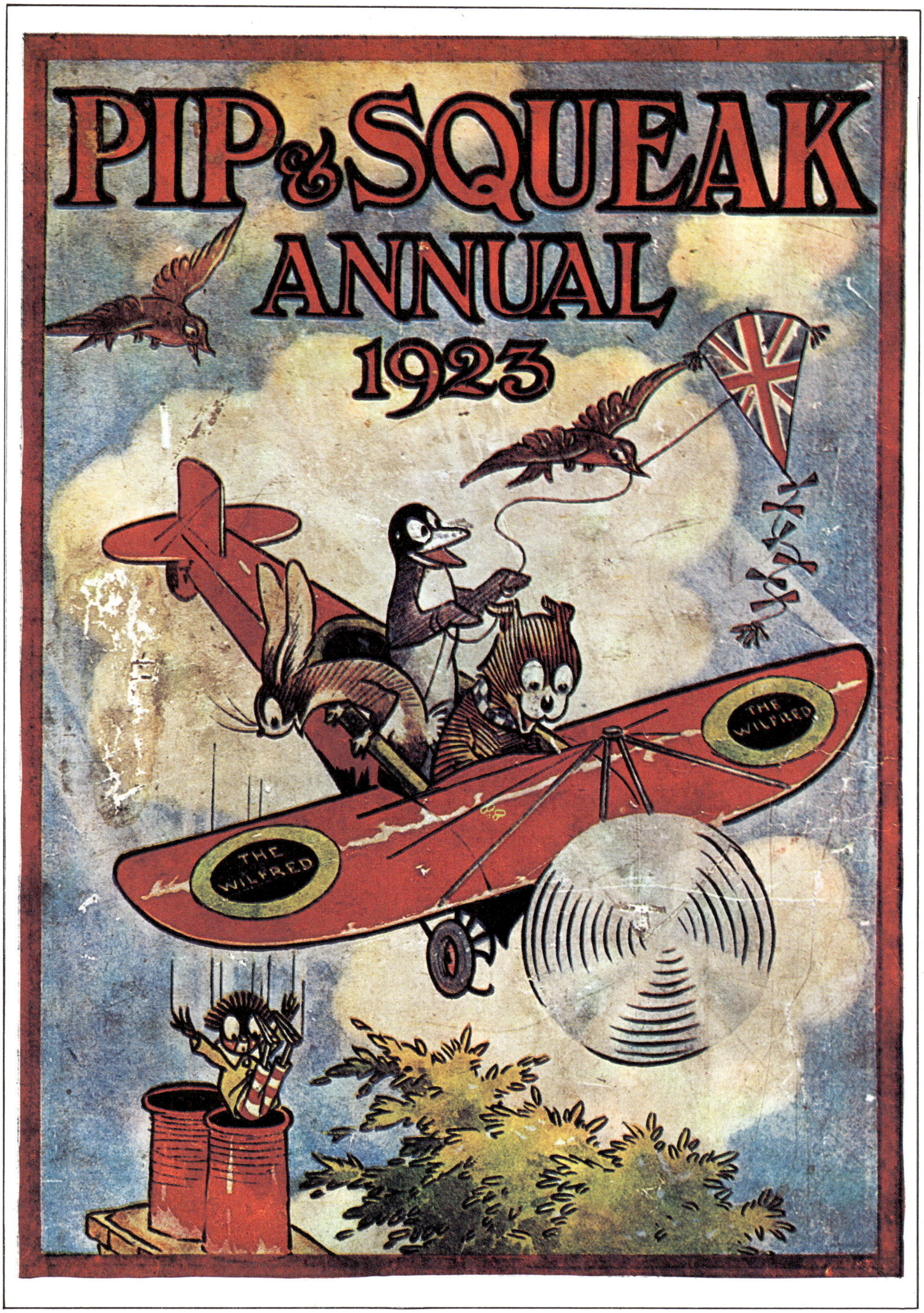

Pinocchio

'There are no strings on me' sang this little woodenhead, who was turned into a real boy by the Blue Fairy when he wished upon a star. Pinocchio also narrowly missed being turned into a donkey after taking a forbidden trip to Pleasure Island. Created by Carlo Collodi in his book of 1881, produced by Walt Disney in his 80-minute film of 1940, Pinocchio's voice was provided by young Dickie Jones.

Pip Squeak & Wilfred

Pip (dog), Squeak (penguin), and Wilfred (rabbit), heroes of one of the earliest and best-loved British newspaper strips (1919), were created by B. J. Lamb and drawn by A. B. Payne. They came to the screen in rather clumsy cut-out cartoons, somnolently animated by Lancelot Speed: *The Wonderful Adventures of Pip, Squeak and Wilfred* (1921).

Pluto

Lolloping flophound of uncertain lineage, yellow-coated – but not yellow-natured at least, not too often – and Mickey Mouse's best friend, Pluto first lent a paw in *The Chain Gang* (1930), a social study directed for Disney by Burt Gillett. Pluto was at his best when opposed by some small creature: a turtle, an armadillo, a gopher. His first solo starring cartoon was *Bone Trouble* (1940) and he won the Oscar for *Lend a Paw* (1941). Farewell appearance: *Pluto's Christmas Tree* (1952).

Police Dog

This canine cop, sometimes referred to as the Pinkerton Pup, was assistant to Officer Piffle of the White Lights Squad. Created by newspaper cartoonist C. T. Anderson, he played the lead in 10 films for John R. Bray's productions during 1914–15.

POPEYE TESTIMONIAL — Popeye, famed one-eyed sailor of the cartoons, is feted by fellow actors at an anniversary party on the Paramount lot in this scene from the spinach-eating strong man's latest Technicolor movie, "Popeye's 20th Anniversary," produced by Famous Studios in celebration of that event this year. Left to right: Jerry Lewis, Dean Martin, Bob Hope (presenting silver spinach cup), Popeye, Olive Oyl and Bing Crosby. The Paramount one-reeler will be released to theatres next month.

Popeye

Asked for a cameo biography, this ancient mariner replied, 'I yam what I yam an' tha's all I yam', adding a pheep through his pipe by way of emphasis. Mighty matelot owing his super-strength to spinach, Popeye the Sailor Man first appeared in *Thimble Theatre*, a newspaper strip by Elzie Crisler Segar, on 17 January 1929. His rapid rise is revealed by the release of his first film appearance, *Popeye the Sailor*, on 14 July 1933. Max Fleischer produced him, Betty Boop introduced him. By 1957 he had starred in 234 cartoons, including the double length *Popeye the Sailor Meets Sinbad the Sailor* (1936) – his only Oscar nomination – and *Popeye the Ace of Space* (1953) – made in three dimensions. His signature song was written by Sammy Timberg and Sam Lerner and was first sung by Billy Costello, alias 'Red Pepper Sam'. Later, scriptwriter Jack Mercer doubled Popeye's voice. King Features eventually produced another 220 Popeye cartoons for television, which took them but two years.

This fluttering star of *Looney Tunes* was the first to utter those Famous Last Words, 'That's all folks!'.

Porky Pig

Created by Bob Clampett as a minor member of the *Merrie Melodies* gang, Porky stuttered his way through 'The M-Midnight Ride of P-Paul R-Revere' in *I Haven't Got a Hat* (1935, director: Friz Freleng). A hesitant star was thus born. Porky replaced the human hero Buddy and shot to fame in *Porky the Rainmaker* (1936, director: Tex Avery). His voice is provided by Mel Blanc. Last titular role: *Porky Chops* (1947), but he continued to oppose Bugs Bunny and Daffy Duck for many a *Merrie Melody*.

e ace color cartoon of 1936-1937

minutes of 3-dimensional laughs... three times footage of the average one-reel cartoon!

MAX FLEISCHER'S

"Sindbad the Sailor"

starring POPEYE

with

Olive Oyl, Wimpy and a great supporting cast. What happens when the spinach-eating seaman—Popeye—gets wrecked on Sindbad's famous tropical island. A short that's going to hit up in the feature picture class in plenty of smart houses.

Two years in the making, and employing all the latest technical developments with sure-fire Popeye starring, prove this absolutely

100%

BOX-OFFICE

Private Snafu

'Situation Normal. All Fouled Up'. Such was the service slogan that gave rise to Private Snafu. This stumble-bum GI was created in 1942 by Theodore Geisel (in peace time known as 'Dr Seuss') for Frank Capra's Army Signal Corps Film Unit. Snafu's series, seen only by soldiers, had such star directors as Frank Tashlin, Chuck Jones and Bob Clampett.

Reluctant Dragon

'Oh, I'm a Reluctant Dragon' he sang (in the voice of Barnett Parker), this tea-sipping, poem-quoting, pot-bellied fellow in green skin. An entire 72-minute feature was named after him, despite his belated appearance in the climactic segment. His battle with Sir Giles, another poetaster, was as phoney as some critics found the film. *The Reluctant Dragon* (1941) was basically a documentary about the Walt Disney studio. (Alan Ladd played an animator!)

Raoul Barré

Influential French animator who created *Animated Grouch Chaser* (1915), a series which interwove cartoons and live action. His first cartoon was *Romiet and Julio* (1915), and later he animated *Mutt and Jeff* (1916).

Quacky Doodles

Quacky Doodles' Picnic (1917) was the first cartoon specifically produced for children. This family of funny ducks was created by Johnny Gruelle, who would later create *Raggedy Ann*. Quacky starred in a series of six pictures.

Road Runner

Lately known as 'Beep Beep' after his tooty type of warning call (given by Paul Julian), this breakneck bird is of the species *Titbitius velocitus*, according to his discoverer, Charles M. (Chuck) Jones. He was first seen (between clouds of dust) in *Fast and Furry-ous* (1948), a Warner Brothers *Looney Tune* written by Michael Maltese, with Wile E. Coyote in hot pursuit.

Robin Hood

This foxy English outlaw and his big bear buddy were on show in *Robin Hood* (1973), the 83-minute Walt Disney Production directed by Wolfgang Reitherman. Created out of ancient British legends by Ken Anderson, Robin's voice was dubbed by Brian Bedford while Little John's came from Phil Harris, and revealed him as coming from the Southern part of Sherwood Forest!

Rollo

Star of *Squirrel War* (1947), this British bushytail predates Ginger Nutt in his technicoloured triumph that ousted Gringo the Grey Squirrel and his bad buddy Brown Rat from Squirrel Wood for ever. *Squirrel War* was one of the last films produced by Anson Dyer, the English animation pioneer.

Sam

'Sam, Sam' was the Infantry man, who refused to 'pick oop' his musket. The immortal ballad by Marriott Edgar, as declaimed by the equally immortal Stanley Holloway, inspired a series of six colour cartoons (England's first), during 1935. Designed and produced by Anson Dyer, *Sam and His Musket* fired the first shot of the series.

Sam Sheepdog

Deadly rival of Ralph Wolf in a series of Chuck Jones cartoons for Warner Brothers, starting with *Steal Wool* (1957). Deadly enemies all day, Sam and Ralph clock off once the whistle blows.

Sammy & Sausage

This small boy and his large dog, were the cartoon creations of Joe Noble, who supplied their short adventures as silent supplements to the *Pathé Pictorial* magazine films issued throughout 1928. Their titles included *Sammy and Sausage On the Moon*.

Scrappy

Help Wanted (1931) was the first cartoon to star the big-eyed boy with a pup called Yippy, who then went on to appear in another 100 titles before 1939. Charles Mintz produced Sid Marcus's creation for Screen Gems, a division of Columbia Pictures. Dick Heumer directed to Joe De Nat's music.

One of Tex Avery's craziest characters, Screwy (spelt 'Skrewy' in his comicbook appearances) took his nutty bow in MGM's *Screwball Squirrel* (1944). His animator was the legendary Preston Blair and his scriptwriter Heck Allen, who later changed his name to Clay Fisher and wrote Western novels instead.

Screwy

The Seven Dwarfs

They dug, dug, dug, dug, dug, dug, dug in a mine the whole day through, then 'Hi-Ho Hi-Ho', it was home from work they went – to find a dragon asleep in three of their beds. When it turned out to be Princess Snow White, their seven stout little hearts prepared to defend her to the death. These knee-high heroes of Walt Disney's historic first feature-length cartoon (83 minutes), *Snow White and the Seven Dwarfs* (1937), were adapted by Ted Sears, Earl Hurd and many others, from the fairy tale by the Brothers Grimm. David Hand supervised several sequence directors including Perce Pearce, Wilfred Jackson and Ben Sharpsteen. The dwarfs returned during the war for a special short made for Canada, *The Seven Wise Dwarfs* (1942).

Doc Bespectacled boss of the band with a spoonerish twist to his speech: 'The lit's light, er, the light's lit.' (Roy Atwell).

Grumpy 'Wimmin is pizen' was his motto, but he turned up trumps in the end (Pinto Colvig).

Happy 'Happy, ma'am, that's me' (Otis Harlan).

Sneezy Based on the explodable comedian Billy Gilbert.

Sleepy Yawned by Pinto Colvig.

Bashful 'Awww gawwsh!' – as he twisted his beard to hide the blushes, was his most characteristic reaction (Scotty Mattraw).

Dopey 'He don't talk none; he never tried!' But he was modelled by an ex-Keystone Kop called Eddie Collins.

Silly Sidney

Fat and foolish, there is some dispute as to whether Silly Sidney should be filed under 'S' or 'Th' since he lisped! Created by Gene Deitch for the *Terrytoons* entitled *Sick Sick Sidney* (1959), this odd elephant's voith was provided by Lionel Watson. Sidney appeared in seven cartoons all told, some of them in Cinemascope.

Silly Symphonies

Skeleton Dance (1929), animated by Ub Iwerks, was the first in the *Billy Symphony* series produced by Walt Disney. The last, *The Ugly Duckling* (1939), won the Oscar. In between came many well-remembered favourites such as *Flowers and Trees* (1932), the first in technicolor, *Who Killed Cock Robin* (1935) and *The Old Mill* (1937). In all 72 *Silly Symphonies* were produced.

Smedly

This western-talking hound dawg with the drawl of Daws Butler provided regular opposition to Chilly Willy the fish-snatching penguin, created by Tex Avery for Walter Lantz and his *Cartunes*.

Sleeping Beauty

This was the colloquial name given to Princess Aurora (alias Briar Rose) after the prick of a cursed needle sent her into somnolence on her sixteenth birthday. Maleficent, the Bad Fairy, was to blame, but gallant Prince Philip saved her with the customary kiss. Walt Disney's most expensive feature (six million dollars), *Sleeping Beauty* (1959) ran 75 minutes and was directed in Technirama by Clyde Geronimi. Her voice was supplied by Mary Costa, while the music came from Tchaikowsky.

Slim & Pim

Slim and Pim, thin and fat respectively, were England's somewhat feeble answer to Mutt and Jeff. Leslie Dowson created them for the Kineto Film Company in a short series of five cartoons beginning with *Allotments* (1918).

RADIO
PICTURES

Sneak Snoop and Snitch

These three sneaky spies, servants of King Bombo of Blefescu do their dirty worst in *Gullivers Travels* (1939). Voices were provided by Jack (Popeye) Mercer and Pinto (Goofy) Colvig. These noisome characters are not Dean Swift's responsibility but were created by Max and Dave Fleischer for their premier feature production.

Sniffles

Sniffles was the cute little mouse with the cute and permanent little cold in the nose. Created by Bob Clampett for *The Night Watchman* (1938), and directed for Warner's *Merrie Melodies* by Chuck Jones, his first title role was *Sniffles and the Bookworm* (1939). Voice and sniffs: Bernice Hanson.

Snoopy

The scene-stealing beagle philosopher came from the *Peanuts* comic strip created by Charles M. Schulz. Having stolen the strip and the first movie version, *A Boy Named Charlie Brown* (1968), the dog went on to star in his own feature film *Snoopy Come Home* (1972). Voice: Director Bill Melendez.

Snookums

When He Wants a Dog He Wants a Dog – this was the then-typical title for the cinematic début of Snookums, spoiled first-born of *The Newlyweds.* This newspaper strip by George McManus was later more suitably titled *Their Only Child.* Emile Cohl, the French creator/animator, made 15 Snookums cartoons in America during 1913–1914. Fortunately, to judge by the graphic yowls, they were all silent!

Snow White

'Some Day My Prince Will Come' she sang confidently (in the voice of Adriana Caselotti), and sure enough he did, for Snow White was not only a Princess in rags, she was the star of the fairy tale by the Brothers Grimm and the world's first full-length (83 minutes) technicolour cartoon. Walt Disney produced *Snow White and the Seven Dwarfs* in 1937 against all advice. David Hand directed, and Marjorie Bell modelled Snow White, later changing her name to Marge Champion.

Space Mouse

Walter Lantz took a flyer at science fiction with this pint-sized protector of the planets who sped around the stratosphere in his Lunar Schooner. *Space Mouse* (1962) was directed by Paul J. Smith and spoken by Johnny Coons. Confusion reigns as Lantz also produced a Hickory, Dickory and Doc cartoon called *Space Mouse* (1964).

Speedy Gonzales

'Arriba! Arriba! Look out, Senor Sylvester, for here comes the fastest mouse in all Mehico. Zip!' And that's Senor Speedy, winning the Senor Oscar on his first ever starring outing, *Speedy Gonzales* (1955). Of course, he had a little help from Senors Friz Freleng (director) and the omnipresent Mel Blanc (voice). Ole!

Spick & Span

The shortlived but stylish stars of one, perhaps more, short cartoon films were produced in 1919 by the popular poster designer and cartoonist of British show business, Victor Hicks.

Spike & Tyke

'Dat's muh boy, over dere, doin' dat!' So boasts proud papa Spike, Brooklyn bulldog, of tiny Tyke, persevering pup, who has treed a jittering Tom to the joy of Jerry. Known previously as Butch the Killer, Spike made a fresh start in *Dog Trouble* (1941), little Tyke first turned up in *Love That Pup* (1949), and the two were promoted to their own series with *Scat Cat* (1956). Created by William Hanna and Joseph Barbera for MGM, these bulldogs were barked by Billy Bletcher.

Splinter & Knothead

What Morty and Ferdy are to Mickey Mouse; Huey, Dewey and Louie to Donald Duck; and Pipeye, Pupeye, Peepeye and Poopeye to Popeye; Splinter and Knothead are to Woody Woodpecker. Their adventures usually involve them in 'new' versions of nursery rhymes such as *Red Riding Hoodlum* (1957). Produced by the *Cartunes* creator Walter Lantz, their voices come from June Foray.

Steve

Perhaps Steve would be more correctly filed under 'C' for 'Come on Steve', the name of his newspaper strip created by Roland Davies. This title came from the cry of the race-going crowd as jockey Steve Donoghue rode to victory after victory. The *Sunday Express* strip was so popular that Davies sunk his savings into a ten-shilling movie camera and launched his own cartoon film company in Ipswich. *Steve Steps Out* (1936) was the first of six funny films, one of its animators being Carl Giles.

Superman

'Look! Up in the sky! Is it a bird? Is it a plane? It's Superman!' Borrowing from the daily radio serial Max Fleischer's animated *Superman* (1941) was launched with this exciting intro, then leapt into action, a comicbook come to life. Animating from the strip hero created by Jerry Seigel and Joe Shuster, Seymour Kneitel, Isidore Sparber, Dave Tendlar and others produced the world's first dramatic cartoon series. In all there were 17 adventures, ending with *Superman in Secret Agent* (1943).

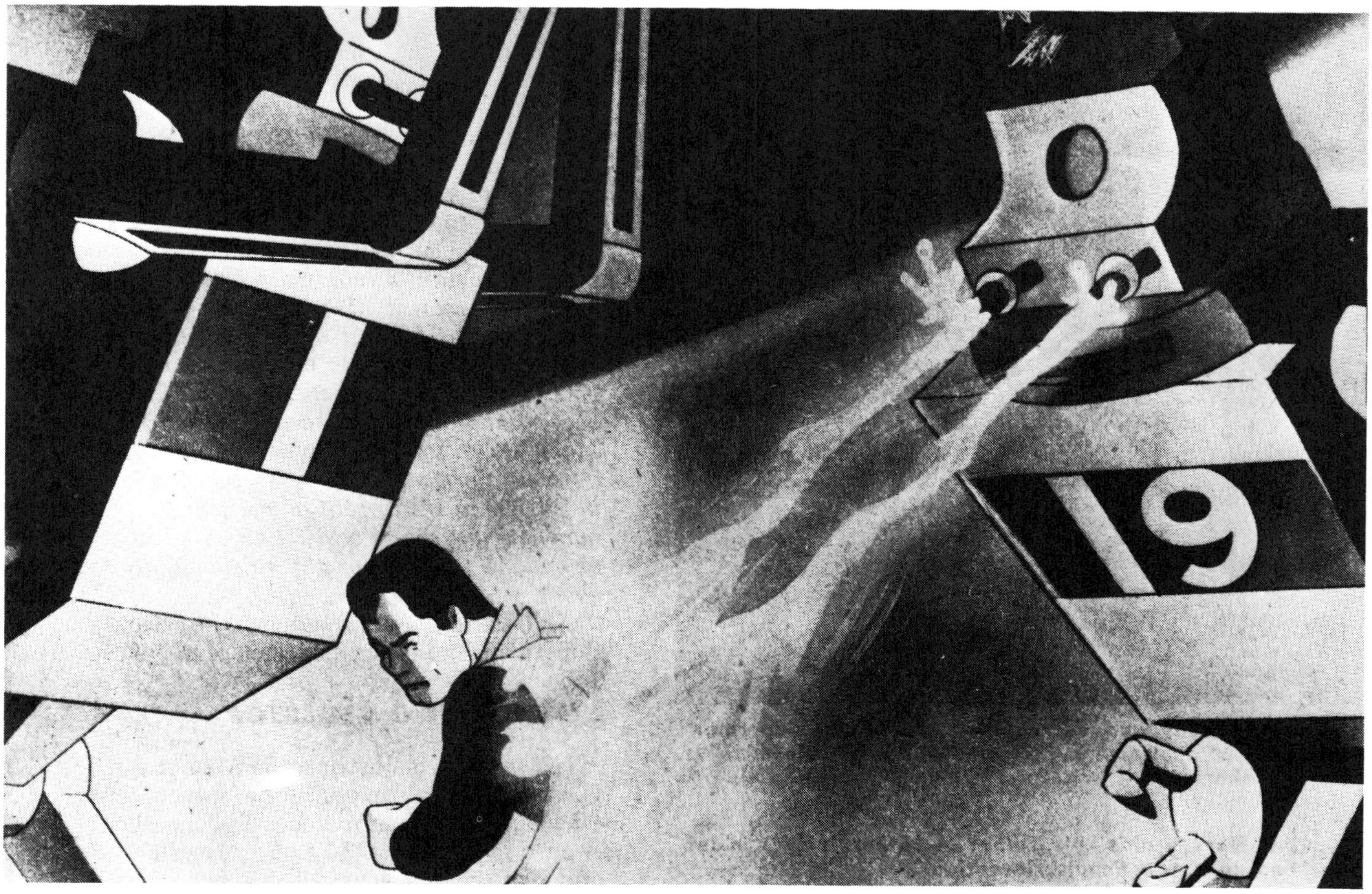

19

55

Swat & Smack

Swat the Fly and Smack the Mosquito – not orders to kill, but names of two supporting insects in Max Fleischer's second feature cartoon *Mr Bug Goes to Town* (1941). They were the hench-insects of the villainous C. Bagley Beetle and were animated by Orestes Calpini.

Sylvester

'Sufferin' succotash!' or more correctly, 'Thufferin' thuccotath!' Sylvester was one of the most complete of the sibilant syllable-slaughterers, and familiar as the Bad Ole Puddy Tat for ever seeking to swallow a little canary bird called Tweetie Pie in such Warner Brothers epics as *A Streetcat Called Sylvester* (1953). Created by Bob McKimson; raspberries blown by the salivating Mel Blanc.

Sylvester Junior

If Spike can have his Tyke, then Sylvester can have his Junior. So reasoned Bob McKimson who gave Sylvester the kitten he proudly calls 'Thon' in *Pop 'Im Pop* (1949). Junior's best buddy is Hippety Hopper, the baby kangaroo who, Sylvester considers, is really a giant mouse. Like his dad, Sylvester Junior speaks with the voice of the unsinkable Mel Blanc.

Tasmanian Devil

'Taz' for short, but not for long, this fast-moving fiend chomped his hungry way into the movies with *Devil May Hare* (1953). Bugs Bunny was Hare while Taz played the Devil. Created by Bob McKimson for Warner Brothers' *Looney Tunes*.

Terry Bears

This cute couple of cubs, players of pranks upon Papa, were part of a *Terrytoons* trio from *Pet Problems* (1954), directed by Connie Rasinski, with voices supplied by Tom Morrison, Philip A. Scheib (normally their music man) and Douglas Moye (Papa). They starred in 16 shorts in all.

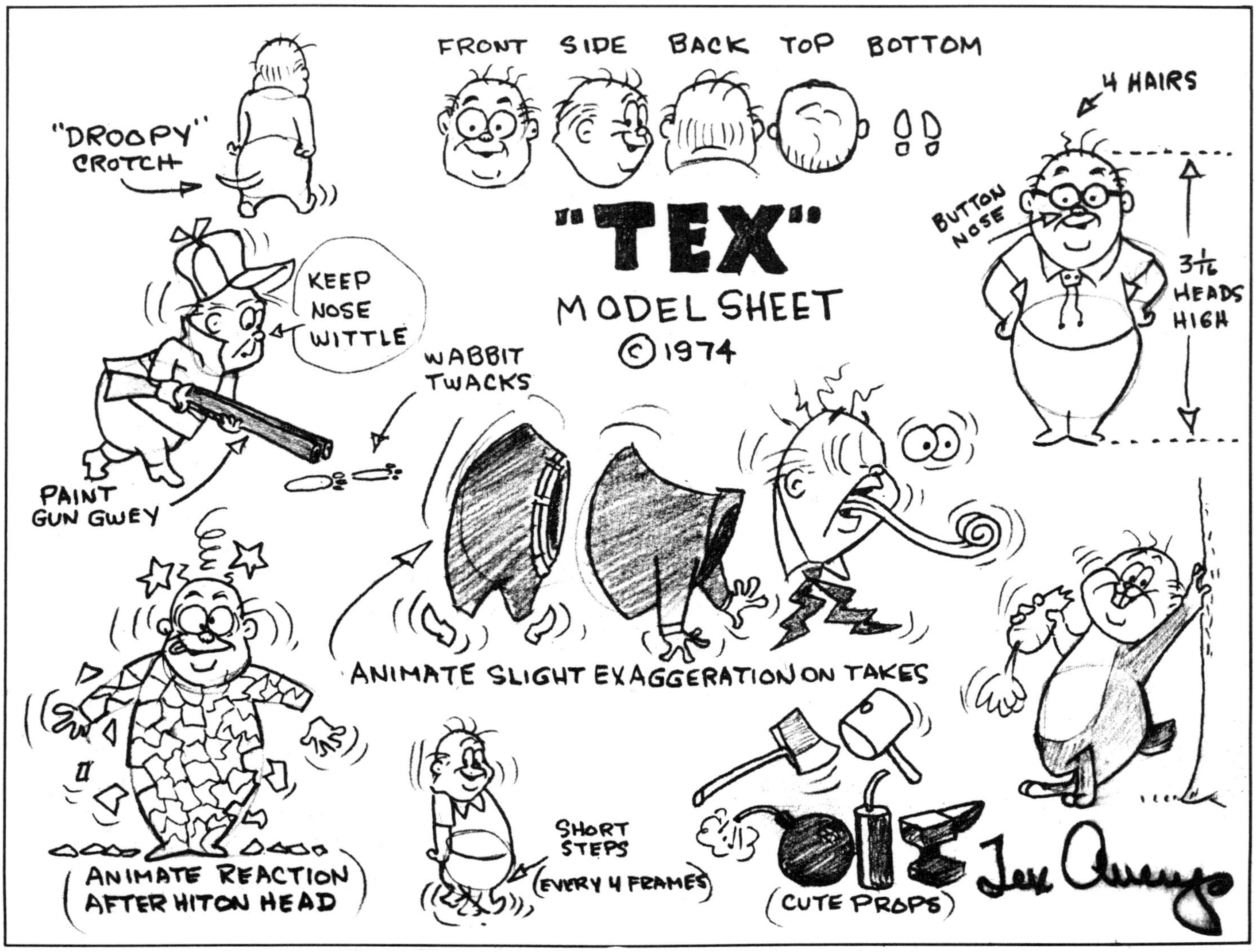

Tex Avery

Frederick Avery, born in Texas 1907, is perhaps the wildest and most way-out gag creator in American animation. He started with Charles Mintz in 1929, and directed *Oswald the Rabbit* for Walter Lantz. Prime periods: Warners (1935–1942) with Porgy Pig and Bugs Bunny; MGM (1942–1955) with Screwly Squirrel and Droopy. Currently in TV commercials.

Thumper

The li'l bunny with an uncontrollably bangy back foot was given to adding his own last lines to his mama's cautionary rhymes. Still, he did teach Prince Bambi to talk: 'Bird . . . Flower . . .' His voice was supplied by Peter Behn, son of one of the animators on Walt Disney's *Bambi* (1942).

Three Caballeros

Parrot, duck and chicken: Joe Carioca, Donald and Panchito. These feathered friends came from the feature film of the same name, a 70-minute Walt Disney production of 1945. Director of cartoons: Norman Ferguson. Director of live action: Harold Young.

Three Little Pigs

As they laughed in the face of the wolf at the door in the Walt Disney *Silly Symphony* short of 1933, a world suffering from economic depression joined in. The baconian brothers promptly won the Oscar, despite the huffing and puffing of their hairy enemy. *The Three Little Pigs* was directed by Burt Gillett, while the stars sang in the voices of Pinto Colvig, Mary Moder and Dorothy Compton. They returned in *The Big Bad Wolf* (1934), *Three Little Wolves* (1936) and *The Practical Pig* (1939), still tooting and fiddling. They also made a special wartime short for Canada called *Thrifty Pig* (1941).

Terrytoons

Series title of the cartoons originated by Paul Terry in 1930. By 1965 over 1,100 cartoons had been made at Terry's studio in New Rochelle. Terry sold his company to the Columbia Broadcasting System, whereupon a 'new look' entered the style under creative director Gene Deitch.

Timothy Mouse

Timothy was the little mouse who befriended a large elephant and ended up as his agent. Timothy was to *Dumbo* (1941) what Jiminy Cricket was to Pinocchio, but slightly more weisenheimer than dogooder. Posed and spoken in best broad Brooklyn by Ed Brophy, buddy of more than one B-movie detective.

Toby Tortoise

Slow but sure hero of the Aesop Fable which Walt Disney turned into a *Silly Symphony* in 1935, *The Tortoise and the Hare*, Toby not only won the race from Max Hare, he won the Academy Award too! This event prompted a Silly Sequel: *Toby Tortoise Returns* (1936). Toby's voice provided by Pinto Colvig.

Tom and Jerry

The original *Tom and Jerry* were humans, fat and thin. They made their debut in *Wot a Night* (1932), a Van Beuren series created by John Foster and George Stallings.

Toby the pup

'A little black beast that walked on its hind legs and had a big mop of black hair.' So director Dick Heumer described sid Marcus' creation Toby. Like so many early cartoon stars he was little more than a moving blot. Made twelve films for Charles Mintz winding up with *The Bull Thrower (1931)*.

Tom & Jerry

The finest if not the first cat and mouse combo in cartoons, Tom and Jerry narrowly missed being called Jasper and Jinx. Thankfully, director Joe Barbera remembered the series he had helped script back in 1932, and they were renamed with the approval of his new partner William Hanna. At MGM their début, produced by Rudolph Ising, was called *Puss Gets the Boot* (1939). It was nominated for the Academy Award which, in due course, Tom and Jerry were to win seven times, from *Yankee Doodle Mouse* (1943) to *Johann Mouse* (1952). They also made two live-action feature appearances: *Anchors Aweigh* (1945), in which Jerry danced with Gene Kelly, and *Dangerous When Wet* (1953), in which they swam with Esther Williams. Their Cinemascope début was *Pet Peeves* (1954), and in all they knocked up a grand total of 154 shorts.

Tom Terrific

Assisted by Mighty Manfred the Wonder Dog, Tom Terrific saved civilisation several times, working from his World Headquarters, a soap-box shed in a tree! Tom was created for the up-dated *Terrytoons* organisation by Gene Deitch and given a voice by Lionel Wilson. Vintage: 1957.

PINES COMICS
CBS Television Presents
APPROVED BY THE COMICS CODE AUTHORITY
Terrytoons
TOM TERRIFIC!
No.1
10¢
CBS
TM CBS Inc.
Boys' Clubs of America
Golden Anniversary Award
presented to
PINES COMICS
For distinguished public service to American youth by publishing comic magazines whose outstanding wholesomeness, interest and entertainment value exemplify the highest publishing standards.
Herbert Hoover, Chairman of the Board
with MIGHTY MANFRED THE WONDER DOG

"I TAUT I TAW A PUDDY-TAT"
(I THOUGHT I SAW A PUSSY CAT)
Introduced in
RECORD RENDEZVOUS
by SAM COSTA
Recorded by
MEL BLANC
ON CAPITOL CL.13407
TWEETY PIE
SYLVESTER
1/-
RMS - CONNELLY LTD.
SELLING AGENTS
PBELL, CONNELLY & Cº LTD.
MADE IN ENGLAND
Featured in WARNER BROS.
"MERRIE MELODIE" Technicolor CARTOON

Tweetie Pie

'I taut I taw a puddy tat a-tweeping up on me,' sang Tweetie Pie, the first cartoon canary to make it to the top of the hit parade. This little yellow fellow won for Warner Brothers their first cartoon Oscar in *Tweetie Pie* (1947), a *Merrie Melody* directed by Friz Freleng. Ten years later, he won another for *Birds Anonymous*. The Bad Ole Puddy Tat a-tweeping up on him was, of course, Sylvester, and their voices were, equally predictably, by the versatile Mel Blanc.

Ugly Duckling

Really a swan all along, this unlucky duck first swam onto the screen in the *Silly Symphony* of 1931. He swam again in 1939, this time in technicolour, and won for Walt Disney an Academy Award. Director: Jack Cutting.

Ub Iwerks

Key figure in the history of American animation, Ub Iwerks (1901–1971), developed *Mickey Mouse* from Walt Disney's original sketches. Animated early Disney series *Alice in Cartoonland*, *Oswald the Rabbit* and *Silly Symphonies* before leaving to create *Flip the Frog* (1931) and *Willie Whopper* (1933). Returned to Disney as Special Effects Supervisor on *20,000 Leagues Under the Sea* (1954).

Willie Walrus

Not easily distinguished from Wally Walrus, unless he has his 'The' with him, Willie the Walrus had the honour of starring in the first *Terrytoon* to be made in Cinemascope. *Arctic Rivals* was produced by veteran animator Paul Terry in 1954.

Wally Walrus

The waddling walrus who talks like early talkie comedian El Brendel turns up from time to time in Woody Woodpecker and Andy Panda *Cartunes* produced for Universal by Walter Lantz. Voice, by yumpin' yiminy, by Dal McKennon.

WARNER BROS. CARTOONS

Walrus & the Carpenter

These were the main protagonists in Bob Hilliar's and Sammy Fain's song 'The Walrus And The Carpenter', based on the poem of the same name by Lewis Carroll, and featured in Walt Disney's *Alice in Wonderland* (1951). Both the Walrus and the Carpenter were spoken by J. Pat O'Malley, Irish actor and well-known walrus and carpenter impersonator.

White Rabbit

He was late, late, for a very important date, and thus had no time to say hello-goodbye, because he was late. Bill Thompson put the panic into the White Rabbit's voice for Walt Disney's version of *Alice in Wonderland* (1951).

Willie the Whale

Originally known as 'the whale who wanted to sing at the Met'!, later christened 'Willie the Operatic Whale', this musical mammal sang 'Figaro', 'Pagliacci' and 'Mephistopheles' before being harpooned to Heaven by Professor Tettitatti. Thanks to the recently wrought miracle of multi-recording, Willie was sung by the many voices of Nelson Eddy. His saga formed the Opera Pathétique' climax to Walt Disney's *Make Mine Music* (1946), supervised by Joe Grant.

WOODY WOODPECKER
BY GEORGE TIBBLES
RAMEY IDRISS
Featured & Broadcast by
DEREK ROY
FROM THE
Walter Lantz
CARTOONS
BY PERMISSION OF WALTER LANTZ
©
PRICE 1/- NET
Leeds Music Ltd
21 DENMARK ST. LONDON. W.C.2

ROAD-RUNNER
AND
COYOTE
PROD-1091
CARRY WHITE BELLY AND NECK

Wile E. Coyote

This desperately determined desert denizen was doomed to disaster despite all the aid the Acme Company could provide for his eternal quest to catch the Road Runner. Created by Chuck Jones for *Fast and Furry-ous* (1948), a Warner Brothers *Looney Tune*, the optimistic animal continued to set traps well into the sixties in such monumental epics as *Run Run Sweet Roadrunner* (1965).

Willie Whopper

Willie was an overweight fantasist, whose imagination worked overtime (along with that of his creator Ub Iwerks) in a series of 13 cartoons produced by the Animated Pictures Corporation. First fancy: *Play Ball* (1933). Wildest dream: *Hell's Fire* (1933) – which so upset the British censor that he had its title changed to *Vulcan Entertains*.

Windy & Breezy

This big bear and little bear duo had no medium-sized go-between. Windy (father) and Breezy (son) are Walter Lantz *Cartune* characters in such shorts as *Three Ring Fling* (1958), which was directed by Paul J. Smith. They speak with the voice of Daws Butler.

Witch Hazel

Wicked old witch featured in *Bewitched Bunny* (1953) and several other Chuck Jones *Looney Tunes*. Cackled by June Foray.

Woody Woodpecker

'Guess who? Ha-ha-ha-ha-ha!' The aggravating woodpecker, who drove Andy Panda mad in *Knock Knock* (1940), returned in the appropriately titled *Woody Woodpecker* (1941). These two scripts by Ben Hardaway and Lowell Elliott set Woody on the tree-lined road to *Cartune* fame and fortune. This Walter Lantz series had spanned 192 films by 1972, making Woody the last of the great cartoon stars. The laughing Mel Blanc recorded the signature tune that shot into the hit parade, but Grace Stafford (Mrs Lantz) was the last of the Woodpeckers.

Winnie Woodpecker

Like Mickey's Minnie, she was Woody's Winnie.

Walter Lantz

Born in New York 1900, newspaper cartoonist Walt Lantz joined Bray Studios in 1922, animating *Katzenjammer Kids*. His first original creations were *Dinky Doodle* (1924) and *Hot Dog Cartoons* (1926) starring Pete the Pup. Took *Oswald the Rabbit* over from Disney (1928), then developed *Cartunes* starring *Andy Panda*, *Woody Woodpecker*, etc.

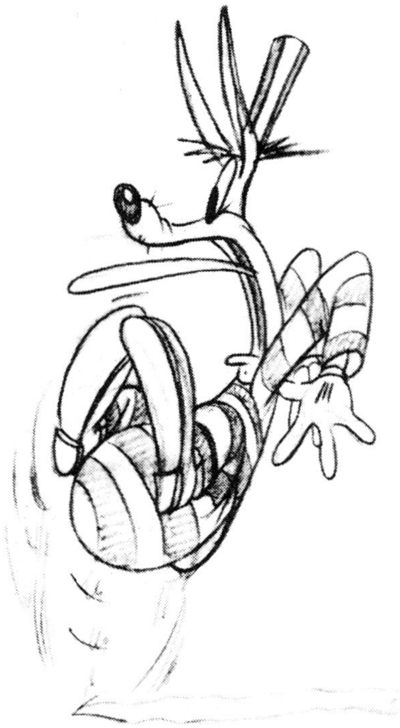

The Wolf

Wild, wacky, way-out character, wolfish in ways undreamed of by the Big Bad Wolf of earlier ilk. Created by Tex Avery for *The Blitz Wolf* (1942), a Hitler burlesque and Avery's first picture for MGM, the Wolf (he never was blessed with a first name) reappeared as the crazy convict of *Dump-Hounded* (1943), Droopy's debut. Final appearance *Homesteader Droopy* (1954). Not to be confused with Ralph Wolf, who clocks on and off with Sam Sheepdog in Chuck Jones' *Steal Wool* (1957).

Wynken Blynken and Nod

Three button-down babies from the old poem written by Eugene Field, they sail the sky in a flying clog and are thunderstruck home to their beds. A Walt Disney *Silly Symphony* from 1938.

Yogi Bear

Unlike the more limited Winnie the Pooh, Yogi was smarter than the average bear, and named by a terrible pun on a bygone baseball star, 'Yogi' Berra. This cheerful raider of 'pic-a-nic' baskets at Jellystone Park is assisted by Booboo, a cautious cub. Created for television by William Hanna and Joseph Barbera, Yogi and Booboo raided the big screen in their feature-length adventure, *Hey There It's Yogi Bear* (1964).

Yogi Bear · The Flintstones · Boss Cat · Huckleberry Hound · Magilla Gorilla · Quick Draw McGraw · Pixie, Dixie and Mr Jinks
FREE GIFT! EVERY WEEK!
No 1
EVERY FRIDAY
HANNA-BARBERA'S
Yogi
AND HIS TOY
10p
FOUR JOLLY ANIMAL STENCILS AND FOUR CRAYONS
FREE INSIDE!
On the centre pages you can read how to use the stencils
AND INSIDE THERE ARE STILL MORE STENCILS YOU CAN MAKE YOURSELF, YOGI.

Zimmy

The cute cub grew up to be the the king of the beasts in *The Lion* (1948). Unimaginatively titled, this was the first of the few *Animaland* cartoons produced in Cookham, England by David Hand, and was directed by Bert Felstead and financed by J. Arthur Rank. The series improved but the money ran out.

Yosemite Sam

Irascible, explodable, sawn-off as a shotgun, this hornswoggled sidewinder six-shot his way into *Bugs Bunny Rides Again* (1947). When next seen he was buckling a swash in *Buccaneer Bunny* (1948). Thereafter there was no holding him. Sam's director was Friz Freleng, his writers Ted Pierce and Michael Maltese, and his swearing was spluttered by the mind-boggling Mel Blanc.

David Hand's
ZIMMY
THE LION
AN Animaland COLOUR CARTOON
STORY
David Hand
CARTOONS

Bibliography

A number of books have been written about animated cartoons, but they are mostly either instruction books on techniques, or studies of Walt Disney. Indeed, this present work seems to be the first attempt at a pictorial history and the first book to approach the genre through its most popular aspect, the cartoon stars. The following Bibliography, necessarily a selective one, lists those books which may prove interesting for further study, but, apart from Leonard Maltin's *The Disney Films*, a prime source for credits, none of them was of any help in the compilation of this book.

Only works in the English language are included, with two singular exceptions, and, furthermore, only those primarily concerned with American and British cartoons. Recommended books are marked with a star. From both the student's and the collector's point of view, the best books on cartoons are those actually adapted from the films themselves. These are generally published as children's books, and as there are so many titles – literally hundreds on Disney films alone – a checklist of these must be left to another time.

* Recommended

BARTON, Jack	*Animating for Fun* USA, 1957.
*BECKER, Stephen	*Comic Art in America* New York, 1959.
*BLAIR, Preston	*Advanced Animation* California, 1949.
*BLOCK, Paul & RITTER, Karl	*Mickey Maus* Berlin, 1937.
*DISNEY, Walt.	*Mickey Mouse Movie Stories* Philadelphia, 1934.
*——	*Sketch Book of Snow White and the Seven Dwarfs* London, 1938.
EPSTEIN, Alvin	*How to Draw Animated Cartoons* New York, 1945.
*FALK, Nat.	*How to Make Animated Cartoons* New York, 1941.
*FIELD, Robert D.	*The Art of Walt Disney* New York, 1944.
*FINCH, Christopher	*The Art of Walt Disney* New York, 1973.
FOSTER, Walter T.	*Animated Cartoons* California, 1947.
*GILLETT, Eric	*Film Fairyland* London, 1948.
GODFREY, Bob	*The Do It Yourself Film Animation Book* London, 1974.
*HALAS, John & HERDEG, Walter	*Film and TV Graphics* Zurich, 1967.
HALAS, John & MANVELL, Roger	*The Technique of Film Animation* London, 1958.
——.	*Art in Movement* London, 1970.
——.	*Design in Motion* London, 1962.
HALAS, John & PRIVETT, Bob	*How to Cartoon for Amateur Films* London, 1958.
KINSEY, Anthony	*Animated Film Making* London, 1970.
KURLAND, G.	*Walt Disney, Master of Animation* New York 1972.
LAUGHTON, Roy	*T.V. Graphics* London, 1966.
LANTZ, Walter	*Easy Way to Draw* Wisconsin, 1958.
LEVITAN, Eli L.	*Animation Art in the Commercial Film* New York, 1960.
*LUTZ, Edwin G.	*Animated Cartoons* New York, 1920.
McCRORY, John R.	*How to Draw for the Movies* Kansas, 1918.
MADSEN, Roy P.	*Animated Film* New York, 1970.
*MALTIN, Leonard	*The Disney Films* New York, 1973.
MANVELL, Roger	*The Animated Film* London, 1954.
MILLER DISNEY, Diane	*Story of Walt Disney* New York, 1957.
*MONDADORI, Arnoldo	*Walt Disney Magic Moments* Milan, 1973.
NOLAN, Bill	*Cartooning Self Taught* London, 1937.
SCHICKEL, Richard	*The Disney Version* New York, 1968.
STEPHENSON, Ralph	*Animation in the Cinema* London, 1967.
——.	*The Animated Film* London, 1973.
*THOMAS, Bob	*Walt Disney: the Art of Animation* New York, 1958.
TURNEY, Harold	*Cartoon Production* California, 1940.

The only periodical concentrating on animated cartoons is *Funnyworld*, edited by Mike Barrier, Box 5229, Brady Station, Little Rock, Arkansas 72205, USA. Those wishing to study cartoons at home will find many available on 16mm and 8mm, sound and mute, colour and monochrome – including Walt Disney Productions, Betty Boop, Bugs Bunny, Felix the Cat, Little Lulu, Popeye, Tom and Jerry, and the Harman-Ising cartoons. A handy guide to, and review of, past releases on 8mm forms a section of my own book, *The Armchair Odeon: The Collector's Guide to The Movies*, published by Fountain Press (1974).

Acknowledgements

For the generous use of his vast files of facts and the generous loan of many of his stills, my special thanks must go to Graham Webb, collector and cartoonist, and dish-washer extraordinary.

The other stills and pictures in this book come from my own collection, but to the original cartoonists and companies concerned, my thanks are also due to, even if many of them are no longer with us.

The rest are arranged alphabetically:

Apple Films; Mike Barrier; Black Ink Films; British Animated Productions; Bob Clampett; C.B.S. Films; Cinema Center Films; Columbia Pictures; Roland Davies; De Patie-Freleng Productions; Anson Dyer Films; H. C. Fisher; Max Fleischer; G.B. Animation; Halas & Batchelor Cartoon Films; Hanna Barbera Productions; Harvey Comics; Chuck Jones; King Features; M.G.M.; National Comics; Joe Noble; Paramount-Famous Studios; RKO-Radio Pictures; Pat Sullivan; Paul Terry; Terrytoons; Twentieth Century Fox; United Features Syndicate; United Productions of America; Universal Pictures; Van Beuren Corporation; Walter Lantz Productions; Warner Brothers-First National-Vitaphone; Western Publishing: Walt Disney Productions.

My apologies to any copyright holder inadvertently unacknowledged.